ITALIAN

Phrase Book & Dictionary

HarperCollins*Publishers*

First published 1990
Copyright © HarperCollins Publishers
Reprint 10 9 8 7 6 5
Printed in Italy by Amadeus SpA, Rome

ISBN 0 00-435870-8

Your *Collins Phrase Book & Dictionary* is a handy, quick-reference guide that will help you make the most of your stay abroad. Its clear layout, with direct alphabetical access to the relevant information, will save you valuable time when you need that crucial word or phrase.

There are two main sections in this book:

* 70 practical topics arranged in A-Z order from **ACCIDENTS** to **WINTER SPORTS** via such subjects as **MENUS**, **ROOM SERVICE** and **TAXIS**. Each topic gives you the basic phrases you will need along with clear but simple pronunciation guidelines. In many cases, there's the added bonus of our 'Streetwise' travel tips – practical and often invaluable travel information.

And, if you've found the right phrase but still need a vital word, you're sure to find it in the final topic, **WORDS**, a brief but rigorously practical list of English words and their translations, chosen for their relevance to the needs of the general traveller.

* A 4000-word foreign vocabulary; the key to all those mystifying but important notices, traffic signs, menus, etc which confront the traveller at every turn. This mini-dictionary will help you enjoy to the full the country's cuisine, save you time when asking directions, and perhaps prevent you getting into one or two tricky situations!

So, just flick through the pages to find the information you require. Why not start with a quick look at the **GRAMMAR**, **ALPHABET** and **PRONUNCIATION** topics? From there on the going is easy with your *Collins Phrase Book & Dictionary*.

Buon viaggio!

LIST OF TOPICS

Streetwise

Third party insurance is obligatory. It is best to carry an international Green Card which you should be able to obtain from your insurers. For a traffic offence the police have the power to fine you on the spot.

There's been an accident	**C'è stato un incidente** *che stahto oon eenchee-**den**tay*
I've crashed my car	**Ho distrutto la macchina** *o dee**stroot**-to la **mak**-keena*
Can I see your insurance certificate, please?	**Posso vedere la sua assicurazione per favore?** *pos-so vay-**day**ray la soo-a as-seekoo-rats-**yoh**nay payr fa-**voh**ray*
We will have to report it to the police	**Dovremo comunicarlo alla polizia** *do-**vray**mo komoo-nee**kahr**-lo al-la poleet see a*
Call the police!	**Chiamate la polizia!** *kee-a-**mah**tay la poleet-**see**-a*
He ran into me	**Mi è venuto contro** *mee e vay-**noo**to kohntro*
I ran into him	**Gli sono andato contro** *lyee sohnoh an-**dah**to kohntroh*
He was driving too fast	**Guidava troppo forte** *gwee-**dah**va trop-po fortay*
He did not give way	**Non ha dato la precedenza** *nohn a dahto la praychay-**dent**sa*
The car number was ...	**La targa era ...** *la tahrga ayra ...*

ACCIDENTS - INJURIES

Streetwise

Carry your passport and your E111 (or other) medical insurance form at all times. There are first aid posts (Pronto Soccorso) at many major railway stations and airports. Dial 113 for ambulance, fire, police.

There has been an accident	**C'è stato un incidente** *che stahto oon eenchee-dentay*
Call an ambulance/ a doctor	**Chiamate un'ambulanza/un dottore** *kee-a-mahtay oonam-boolant-sa/oon doht-tohray*
He has hurt himself	**Si è fatto male** *see e faht-to mahlay*
I am hurt	**Mi sono fatto male** *mee sohnoh faht-to mahlay*
He is seriously injured/bleeding	**È ferito gravemente/Perde sangue** *e fay-reeto grahvay-mayntay/payrday san-gway*
He can't breathe/ move	**Non può respirare/muoversi** *nohn pwo rayspee-rahray/mwo-vayrsee*
I can't move my arm/leg	**Non posso muovere il braccio/la gamba** *nohn pos-so mwo-vayray eel brat-cho/ la gamba*
Cover him up	**Copritelo** *kopree-telo*
Don't move him	**Non muovetelo** *nohn mwovay-telo*
He has broken his arm/cut himself	**Ha rotto il braccio/Si è tagliato** *a rot-to eel brat-cho/see e tal-yahto*

See also **EMERGENCIES**

Streetwise

Hotels are officially graded from one to five stars, while boarding houses (pensioni) are grouped into three categories. Prices are usually per room and normally include a 17% service charge and IVA (VAT).

I want to reserve a single/double room	**Vorrei prenotare una camera singola/ matrimoniale** *vor-**re**-ee prayno-**tah**ray oona **ka**-mayra **seen**-gohla/matree-mohn-**yah**lay*
Is there a restaurant/bar?	**C'è un ristorante/bar?** *che oon reesto-**ran**tay/bar*
I want bed and breakfast/full board	**Vorrei una camera con prima colazione/ pensione completa** *vor-**re**-ee oona **ka**-mayra kohn preema kolats **yoh**nay/paynsee-**oh**nay komple**ta*
What is the daily/ weekly rate?	**Quanto costa al giorno/alla settimana?** *kwanto kohsta al jorno/al-la sayt-tee-**mah**na*
Is breakfast included in the price?	**La colazione è compresa nel prezzo?** *la kolats-**yoh**nay e kom-**pray**za nel pret-so*
I want to stay three nights/from ... till ...	**Voglio restare per tre notti/dal ... fino al ...** *vol-yo rays-**tah**ray payr tray not-tee/ dal ... feeno al ...*
We'll be arriving at ...	**Arriveremo alle ...** (see TIME) *ar-reevay-**ray**mo al-lay ...*
Shall I confirm by letter?	**Devo mandare una conferma scritta?** *dayvo man-**dah**ray oona kon-**fayr**ma skreet-ta*

See also **HOTEL DESK, ROOM SERVICE, SELF-CATERING**

Where do I check in for the flight to Milan?	**Dov'è il check-in del volo per Milano?** *dohve eel check in del vohloh payr meelahno*
Which departure gate do I go to?	**A quale uscita devo andare?** *a kwahlay oo-sheeta dayvo an-dahray*
I'd like an aisle/ a window seat	**Vorrei un posto centrale/vicino al finestrino** *vor-re-ee oon pohstoh chayn-trahlay/ vee-cheeno al feenes-treeno*
Will a meal be served on the plane?	**Daranno da mangiare sull'aereo?** *daranno da man-jahray sool-la-e-ray-o*
Where is the snack bar/duty-free shop?	**Dov'è il bar/duty free?** *dohve eel bar/duty free*
Where can I change some money?	**Dove posso cambiare i soldi?** *dohvay pos-so kamb-yahray ee soldee*
Where do I get the bus to town?	**Dove posso prendere l'autobus per la città?** *dohvay pos-so pren-dayray low-toboos payr la cheet-ta*
Where are the taxis/telephones?	**Dove sono i taxi/telefoni?** *dohvay sohnoh ee taksee/tayle-fonee*
I want to hire a car/reserve a hotel room	**Vorrei noleggiare una macchina/ prenotare una stanza** *vor-re-ee nolayd-jahray oona mak-keena/ prayno-tahray oona stantsa*
I am being met	**Mi stanno aspettando** *mee stan-no aspayt-tando*

The Italian alphabet is the same as the English although native Italian words lack J, K, W, X and Y. The pronunciation of each letter is given below together with the word used conventionally for clarification when spelling something out.

A *a*	**come** *koh-may*	**Ancona** *an-kohna*	**N** *en-ne*	**come** *koh-may*	**Napoli** *nahpolee*
B *bee*	**for**	**Bari** *bah-ree*	**O** *o*	**for**	**Otranto** *o-tranto*
C *chee*		**Catania** *katahnee-a*	**P** *pee*		**Palermo** *palayr-mo*
D *dee*		**Domodossola** *domo-dos-sola*	**Q** *koo*		**quarto** *kwar-to*
E *ay*		**Empoli** *em-polee*	**R** *er-re*		**Roma** *roh-ma*
F *ef-fe*		**Firenze** *fee-rent-say*	**S** *es-se*		**Savona** *savoh-na*
G *jee*		**Genova** *jenovah*	**T** *tee*		**Torino** *toree-no*
H *ak-ka*		**Hotel** *oh tol*	**U** *oo*		**Udine** *oodee-nay*
I *ee*		**Imperia** *eem-payree-a*	**V** *voo*		**Venezia** *vaynayt-see-a*
J *ee loon-goh*			**W** *dop-pee-ohvoo*		
K *kap-pa*			**X** *eex*		
L *el-le*		**Livorno** *lee-vorno*	**Y** *ee gre-koh*		
M *em-me*		**Milano** *mee-lahno*	**Z** *dze-ta*		

ASKING QUESTIONS

Streetwise

When addressing someone you are not on familiar terms with you should always use the pronoun Lei and the third person singular part of the verb. Thus, 'Are you the hotel manager?' translates as 'Lei è il padrone dell'albergo?' *(le-ee e eel pa-drohnay del-lal-bayrgo).*

Is it far/expensive?	**È lontano/costa molto?** *e lon-tahno/kohsta mohltoh*
Do you understand?	**Ha capito?** *a ka-peeto*
Can you help me?	**Può aiutarmi?** *pwo a-yoo-tahrmee*
Where are the shops?	**Dove sono i negozi?** *dohvay sohnoh ee nay-gotsee*
When will it be ready?	**Quando sarà pronto?** *kwando sara prohnto*
How do I get there?	**Come faccio per andarci?** *kohmay fat-cho payr an-dahrchee*
How far/big is it?	**Quanto è distante/grande?** *kwanto e dee-stantay/granday*
Is there a good restaurant?	**C'è un buon ristorante?** *che oon bwon reesto-rantay*
What is this?	**Che cos'è questo?** *kay koze kwaysto*
How much is it?	**Quanto costa?** *kwanto kohsta*

Streetwise

At many beaches in Italy you will be expected to pay for the use of cabins, beach umbrellas and deck-chairs. Such beaches normally have a bar and are frequently patrolled by a lifeguard (bagnino). There will usually be an area of the beach without facilities which can be used free of charge. A red flag means that it is unsafe to swim in the sea.

Is it dangerous to swim here?	**È pericoloso nuotare qui?** *e payree-ko-**loh**zo nwo-**tah**ray kwee*
When is high/low tide?	**Quando c'è l'alta/la bassa marea?** *kwando che lalta/la bas-sa ma-**ray**-a*
How deep is the water?	**Quanto è profonda l'acqua?** *kwanto e pro-**fohn**da lakwa*
Are there strong currents?	**Ci sono correnti forti?** *chee sohnoh kor-**rayn**tee fortee*
Is it a private/ quiet beach?	**È una spiaggia privata/tranquilla?** *e oona spee-**ad**-ja pree-**vah**ta/tran**kweel**-la*
Where do we change?	**Dove sono gli spogliatoi?** *dohvay sohnoh lyee spol-yato-ee*
Can I hire a deck chair?	**Posso prendere in affitto una sedia a sdraio?** *pos-so **pren**-dayray een af-**feet**to oona sed-ya a zdra-yo*
Can I go fishing?	**Posso andare a pescare?** *pos-so an-**dah**ray a pay-**skah**ray*
Is there a children's pool?	**C'è una piscina per bambini?** *che oona pee-**shee**na payr bam-**bee**nee*

BREAKDOWNS

Streetwise

If you breakdown dial 116 for the ACI (Automobile Club d'Italia) which is affiliated to the AA and the RAC. Their nearest office will be informed and assistance will be sent as soon as possible. Motorists must carry a red warning triangle. This should be placed 50 m behind your vehicle before seeking help. There are emergency phones along the motorways at 1 km intervals.

My car has broken down

La mia macchina si è rotta
*la mee-a **mak**-keena see e roht-ta*

There is something wrong with the brakes/the electrics

C'è qualcosa che non va nei freni/ nell'impianto elettrico
*che kwal-**ko**za kay nohn va nay-ee fraynee/nel-leemp-**yan**to ay**let**-treeko*

I have run out of petrol

Sono rimasto senza benzina
*sohnoh ree-**mas**to sentsa bend-**zee**na*

There is a leak in the petrol tank/ radiator

Il serbatoio/radiatore perde
*eel sayrba-**to**yo/rad-ya-**toh**ray payrday*

The windscreen has shattered

Il parabrezza si è rotto
*eel para-**braydz**-za see e roht-to*

The engine is overheating

Il motore è surriscaldato
*eel moh-**toh**ray e soor-reeskal-**dah**to*

Can you tow me to a garage?

Può trainarmi da un meccanico?
*pwo tra-ee-**nahr**mee da oon mayk-**ka**-neeko*

Can you send a mechanic/a breakdown van?

Può mandare un meccanico/un carro attrezzi?
*pwo man-**dah**ray oon mayk-**ka**neeko/oon kar-ro at-**trayts**-see*

Streetwise

Office hours vary but most offices will be open from 0830-1230 and then from 1530-1930, Mon.-Fri. Government offices are open from 0830-1400, Mon.-Sat.

I have an appointment with Signor Simone	**Ho un appuntamento con il Signor Simone** *o oon ap-poonta-maynto kohn eel seen-yor see-mohnay*
He is expecting me	**Mi sta aspettando** *mee sta aspayt-tando*
Can I leave a message with his secretary?	**Posso lasciare un messaggio alla sua segretaria?** *pos-so la-shahray oon mays-sad-jo al-la soo-a saygray-tar-ya*
I am free tomorrow morning/for lunch	**Sono libero domani mattina/per pranzo** *sohnoh lee-bayro do-mahnee mat-teena/ payr prantso*
Can I send a telex from here?	**Posso mandare un telex da qui?** *pos-so man-dahray oon telex da kwee*
Where can I get some photocopying done?	**Dove posso far fare delle fotocopie?** *dohvay pos-so fahr fahray dayl lay foto-kop-yay*
I want to send this by courier	**Voglio spedire questo tramite corriere** *vol-yo spay-deeray kwaysto tra-meetay kor-ree-e-ray*
Have you a catalogue/some literature?	**Avete un catalogo/del materiale informativo?** *a-vaytay oon kata-logo/del matayr-yahlay eenfor-ma-teevo*

BUYING

Streetwise

Do you sell stamps?	**Vende francobolli?** *vaynday frankoh-**bohl**-lee*
How much is that?	**Quanto costa quello?** *kwanto kohsta kwayl-lo*
Have you anything smaller/bigger?	**Avete qualcosa di più piccolo/di più grande?** *a-**vay**tay kwal-**ko**za dee pee-oo **peek**-kolo/ dee pee-oo granday*
Have you got any bread/matches?	**Avete del pane/dei fiammiferi?** *a-**vay**tay del pahnay/day-ee fee-am-**mee**-fayree*
I'd like a newspaper/ some apples	**Vorrei un giornale/delle mele** *vor-**re**-ee oon jor-**nah**lay/dayl-lay maylay*
I prefer this one	**Preferisco questo** *prayfay-**rees**ko kwaysto*
I'd like to see the one in the window	**Vorrei vedere quello in vetrina** *vor-**re**-ee vay-**day**ray kwayl-lo een vay-**tree**na*
I'll take this one/ that one there	**Prendo questo/quello là** *prendo kwaysto/kwayl-lo la*
Could you wrap it up for me please?	**Può incartarlo per favore?** *pwo eenkahr-**tahr**lo payr fa-**voh**ray*

See also **MEASUREMENTS, PAYING, SHOPPING**

Streetwise

There are numerous official camping sites with excellent facilities, sometimes including a restaurant and store. Never camp without permission in fields or on common land, as penalties are severe. Tourist offices will provide details of the facilities in their area.

We are looking for a camp site	**Stiamo cercando un campeggio** *stee-**ah**mo chayr-**kan**do oon kam**payd**-jo*
Do you have any vacancies?	**Avete dei posti liberi?** *a-**vay**tay day-ee pohstee **lee**-bayree*
How much is it per night?	**Quanto costa per notte?** *kwanto kohsta payr not-tay*
We want to stay one week	**Vogliamo restare per una settimana** *vol-**yah**mo rays-**tah**ray payr oona sayt-tee-**mah**na*
May we camp here?	**Possiamo campeggiare qui?** *pos-**yah**mo kampayd-**jah**ray kwee*
Is there a more sheltered/secluded site?	**C'è un posto più riparato/appartato?** *che oon pohstoh pee-oo reepa-**rah**to/ap-par**tah**to*
Can we park our caravan there?	**Possiamo mettere là la nostra roulotte?** *pos-**yah**mo **mayt**-tayray la la nostra roo**lot***
Is there a shop/restaurant on the site?	**C'è uno spaccio/un ristorante nel campeggio?** *che oono spat-cho/oon reesto-**ran**tay nayl kam**payd**-jo*
Where is the washroom/drinking water?	**Dov'è il bagno/l'acqua potabile?** *doh**ve** eel ban-yo/lakwa po**tah**-beelay*

CAR HIRE

Streetwise

Cars can be hired in most towns and at airports and main railway stations. You must be at least 21 and have held a full licence for a year. Prices normally include maintenance, breakdown service and basic insurance while petrol and any additional insurance are extra. Some companies will only take credit cards as payment.

I want to hire a car	**Voglio noleggiare una macchina** *vol-yo nolayd-jahray oona mak-keena*
I need a car with a chauffeur	**Mi occorre una macchina con autista** *mee ok-koh-ray oona mak-keena kohn ow-teesta*
I want a large/ small car	**Voglio una macchina grande/piccola** *vol-yo oona mak-keena granday/peek-kola*
Is there a charge per kilometre?	**Bisogna pagare secondo il chilometraggio?** *beezohn-ya pa-gahray say-kohndoh eel keelo-maytrad-jo*
How much extra is the comprehensive insurance cover?	**Quant'è il supplemento per l'assicurazione che copre tutti i rischi?** *kwan-te eel sooplay-maynto payr lasee-koorats-yohnay kay kohpray toot-tee ee reeskee*
I would like to leave the car in Rome	**Vorrei lasciare la macchina a Roma** *vor-re-ee lashahray la mak-keena a rohma*
My husband/wife will be driving as well	**Anche mio marito/mia moglie guiderà** *ankay mee-o ma-reeto/mee-a mohl-yay gweeday-ra*
How do I operate the controls?	**Come funzionano i comandi?** *kohmay foontsee-oh-nano ee ko-mandee*

CHEMIST'S

Streetwise

Chemists in Italy operate a rota system whereby at least one chemist's (farmacia) in each area is open outside normal shop hours. Details are displayed at every chemist's under the heading ore di turno. Some prescribed medicines are free while others carry a small charge, but you must show your E111 form to the chemist.

I want something for a headache/a sore throat/ toothache	**Voglio qualcosa per il mal di testa/mal di gola/mal di denti** *vol-yo kwal-koza payr eel mal dee testa/mal dee gohla/mal dee dentee*
I would like some sticking plaster	**Vorrei dei cerotti** *vor-re-ee day-ee chayrot-tee*
Have you anything for insect bites/ sunburn?	**Avete qualcosa per le punture di insetti/ scottature solari?** *a-vaytay kwal-koza payr lay poon-tooray dee eenset-tee/skot-ta-tooray so-lahree*
I have a cold/a cough	**Ho il raffreddore/la tosse** *o eel raf-frayd-dohray/la tohs-say*
Is this suitable for an upset stomach?	**Questo va bene per dei disturbi allo stomaco?** *kwaysto va benay payr day-ee dee stoorbee al-lo sto-mako*
How much/how many do I take?	**Quanto/quanti ne devo prendere?** *kwanto/kwantee nay dayvo pren-dayray*
How often do I take it?	**Ogni quante ore devo prenderlo?** *on-yee kwantay ohray dayvo pren-dayrlo*
I have a prescription from a doctor	**Ho una ricetta del dottore** *o oona reechayt-ta dayl doht-tohray*

CHILDREN

Streetwise

Children are normally well catered for in Italy and are welcome everywhere including bars and restaurants. There are many reductions available on transport, in hotels, etc. Check with the local tourist office for details.

I have a small baby/ two children

Ho un bambino piccolo/due bambini
o oon bam-beeno peek-kolo/doo-ay bam-beenee

Do you have a special rate for children?

Avete delle riduzioni per bambini?
a-vaytay dayl-lay reeduts-yohnee payr bam-beenee

Do you have facilities/activities for children?

Avete dei servizi/Organizzate delle attività per bambini?
a-vaytay day-ee sayr-veetsee/orga-needz-zahtay day-lay at-teevee-ta payr bam-beenee

Have you got a cot for the baby?

Avete un lettino per il bambino?
a-vaytay oon layt-teeno payr eel bam-beeno

Where can I feed/ change the baby?

Dove posso allattare/cambiare il bambino?
dohvay pos-so al-lat-tahray/kamb-yahray eel bam-beeno

Where can I warm the baby's bottle?

Dove posso riscaldare il biberon?
dohvay pos-so reeskal-dayray eel beebay-ron

Is there a playroom?

C'è una stanza giochi?
che oona stantsa jokee

Is there a baby-sitting service?

C'è un servizio di babysitter?
che oon sayr-veets-yo dee babysitter

CHURCH & WORSHIP

Streetwise

Visitors to churches should always be suitably dressed, even if they are only there as tourists. Shorts, short skirts and even short sleeves are often considered disrespectful and visitors so attired could even find themselves being asked to leave.

Where is the nearest church?	**Dov'è la chiesa più vicina?** *dohve la kee-e-za pee-oo vee-cheena*
Where is there a Protestant church?	**Dove posso trovare una chiesa protestante?** *dohvay pos-so tro-vahray oona kee-e-za protay-stantay*
I want to see a priest	**Voglio vedere un prete** *vol-yo vay-dayray oon pre-tay*
What time is the service?	**A che ora è la messa?** *a kay ohra e la mays-sa*
I want to go to confession	**Voglio andare a confessarmi** *vol-yo an-dahray a konfays-sahrmee*

CITY TRAVEL

Streetwise

Bus and tram tickets can be bought at tobacconists' (tabaccherie), newspaper kiosks and in many bars. Once on the bus/tram you must immediately stamp your ticket in a machine which is normally situated near the door. In many towns the ticket is then valid for an hour and can be used within that time on other buses/trams.

Does this bus/
train go to ...?

Quest'autobus/treno va a ...?
kwaystow-toboos/treno va a ...

Which number bus
goes to ...?

Quale autobus va a ...?
kwahlay ow-toboos va a ...

Where do I get a
bus for the airport/
cathedral?

Da dove parte l'autobus per l'aeroporto/il duomo?
da dohvay partay low-toboos payr la-ayro-porto/ eel dwomo

Where do I change/
get off?

Dove devo cambiare/scendere?
dohvay dayvo kamb-yahray/shayn-dayray

How frequent are
the buses/trains
to town?

Ogni quanto ci sono gli autobus/i treni per la città?
on-yee kwanto chee sohnoh lyee ow-toboos/ee trenee payr la cheet-ta

What is the fare to
the town centre?

Qual'è la tariffa per andare in centro?
kwahle la tareef-fa payr an-dahray een chentro

Where do I buy a
ticket?

Dove posso comprare il biglietto?
dohvay pos-so kom-prahray eel beel-yayt-to

What time is the
last bus?

Quando parte l'ultimo autobus?
kwando partay lool-teemo ow-toboos

Is there a laundry service?	**C'è un servizio di lavanderia?** *che oon sayrveets-yo dee lavan-dayree-a*
Is there a launderette/dry cleaner's nearby?	**C'è una lavanderia automatica/lavanderia a secco qui vicino?** *che oona lavan-dayree-a owto-ma-teeka/lavan-dayree-a sayk-ko kwee vee-cheeno*
Where can I get this skirt cleaned/ironed?	**Dove posso far pulire/stirare questa gonna?** *dohvay pos-so fahr poo-leeray/stee-rahray kwaysta gon-na*
Where can I do some washing?	**Dove posso fare del bucato?** *dohvay pos-so fahray dayl boo-kahto*
I need some soap and water	**Mi occorre acqua e sapone** *mee ohk kohr-ray akwa ay sa-pohnay*
Where can I dry my clothes?	**Dove posso far asciugare i vestiti?** *dohvay pos-so fahr ashoo-gahray ee vay-steetee*
This stain is coffee	**Questa è una macchia di caffè** *kwaysta e oona mak-ya dee kaf-fe*
Can you remove this stain?	**Può smacchiare questo?** *pwo zmak-yahray kwaysto*
This fabric is very delicate	**Questa stoffa è molto delicata** *kwaysta stof-fa e mohltoh daylee-kahta*
When will my things be ready?	**Quando saranno pronte le mie cose?** *kwando saran-no prontay lay mee-ay kozay*

CLOTHES

I take a size ...	**Porto la misura ...**
	porto la mee-zoora ...
Can you measure me please?	**Può prendermi le misure?**
	pwo pren-dermee lay mee-zooray
May I try on this dress?	**Posso provare questo vestito?**
	pos-so pro-vahray kwaysto vay-steeto
May I take it over to the light?	**Posso vederlo alla luce?**
	pos-so vay-dayrlo al-la loochay
Where are the changing rooms?	**Dove sono gli spogliatoi?**
	dohvay sohnoh lyee spolyah-to-ee
Is there a mirror?	**C'è uno specchio?**
	che oono spek-yo
It's too big/small	**È troppo grande/piccolo**
	e trop-po granday/peek-kolo
What is the material?	**Che stoffa è?**
	kay stof-fa e
Is it washable?	**È lavabile?**
	e lavah-beelay
I don't like it/ them	**Non mi piace/piacciono**
	nohn mee pee-achay/pee-at-chono
I don't like the colour	**Non mi piace il colore**
	nohn mee pee-achay eel koh-lohray

COACH TRAVEL

Streetwise

Italians refer to a coach either as un pullman *(oon pool-man) or as* un autobus *(oon **ow**-toboos).*

| Is there a bus to ...? | **C'è un autobus per ...?** |
| | *che oon **ow**-toboos payr ...* |

| Which bus goes to ...? | **Quale autobus va a ...?** |
| | *kwahlay **ow**-toboos va a ...* |

| Where do I catch the bus for ...? | **Dove posso prendere l'autobus per ...?** |
| | *dohvay pos-so **pren**-dayray **low**-toboos payr ...* |

| What are the times of the buses to ...? | **Quando partono gli autobus per ...?** |
| | *kwando **pahr**-tono lyee **ow**-toboos payr ...* |

| Does this bus go to ...? | **Quest'autobus va a ...?** |
| | *kway**stow**-toboos va a ...* |

| Where do I get off? | **Dove devo scendere?** |
| | *dohvay dayvo **shayn**-dayray* |

| Is there a toilet on board? | **C'è una toilette sull'autobus?** |
| | *che oona twa**let** sool **low**-toboos* |

| Is there an overnight service to ...? | **C'è un servizio notturno per ...?** |
| | *che oon sayr-**veets**-yo not-**toorn**o payr ...* |

| What time does it leave/arrive? | **A che ora parte/arriva?** |
| | *a kay ohra partay/ar-**ree**va* |

| Will you tell me where to get off? | **Mi può dire quando devo scendere?** |
| | *mee pwo deeray kwando dayvo **shayn**-dayray* |

| Let me off here, please | **Mi faccia scendere qui, per favore** |
| | *mee fat-cha **shayn**-dayray kwee payr fa-**voh**ray* |

COMPLAINTS

This does not work	**Questo non funziona** *kwaysto nohn foonts-yohna*
I can't turn the heating off/on	**Non riesco a spegnere/ad accendere il riscaldimento** *nohn ree-esko a spayn-yayray/ad at-chendayray eel reeskal-dee-maynto*
The lock is broken	**La serratura è rotta** *la sayr-ra-toora e roht-ta*
I can't open the window	**Non riesco ad aprire la finestra** *nohn ree-esko ad a-preeray la fee-nestra*
The toilet won't flush	**Non esce acqua dal water** *nohn e-shay ak-kwa dal vatayr*
There is no hot water/toilet paper	**Non c'è acqua calda/carta igienica** *nohn che ak-kwa kalda/kahrta ee-je-neeka*
The washbasin is dirty	**Il lavandino è sporco** *eel lavan-deeno e sporko*
My coffee is cold	**Il caffè è freddo** *eel kaf-fe e fred-do*
We are still waiting to be served	**Stiamo ancora aspettando di essere serviti** *stee-ahmo an-kohra aspayt-tando dee es-sayray sayr-veetee*
I bought this here yesterday	**Questo l'ho comprato qui ieri** *kwaysto lo kom-prahto kwee ye-ree*
It has a flaw/hole in it	**È difettoso/bucato** *e deefayt-tohzo/boo-kahto*

Streetwise

Italians shake hands more frequently when they meet than people do in Britain.

How do you do?/ Hello/Goodbye	**Piacere!/Buon giorno/Arrivederci** *pee-a-chayray/bwon jorno/ar-reevay dayrchee*
Do you speak English?	**Parla inglese?** *parla een-glayzay*
I don't speak Italian	**Non parlo italiano** *nohn parlo eetal-yahno*
What's your name?	**Come si chiama?** *komay see kee-ahma*
My name is ...	**Mi chiamo ...** *mee kee-ahmo ...*
Do you mind if I sit here?	**Le dispiace se mi siedo qui?** *lay deespee-achay say mee see-e-do kwee*
I'm English/Irish/ Scottish/Welsh	**Sono inglese/irlandese/scozzese/gallese** *sohnoh een-glayzay/eerlan-dayzay/skots-sayzay/ gal-layzay*
Are you Italian?	**Lei è italiano?** *le-ee eetal-yahno*
Where do you come from?	**Da dove viene?** *da dohvay vee-e-nay*
Would you like a cup of coffee/a drink?	**Gradisce un caffè/qualcosa da bere?** *gra-deeshay oon kaf-fe/kwal-koza da bayray*

See also **GREETINGS**

CONVERSATION 2

Yes please/No thank you	**Sì grazie/No grazie** *see grats-yay/no grats-yay*
Thank you (very much)	**(Molte) grazie** *(mohltay) grats-yay*
Don't mention it	**Prego** *praygo*
I'm sorry	**Mi dispiace** *mee deespee-achay*
I'm on holiday here	**Sono qui in vacanza** *sohnoh kwee een va-kantsa*
This is my first trip to ...	**Questo è il mio primo viaggio a ...** *kwaysto e eel mee-o preemo vee-ad-jo a ...*
Do you mind if I smoke?	**Le dispiace se fumo?** *lay deespee-achay say foomo*
Would you like a drink?	**Vuole qualcosa da bere?** *vwolay kwal-koza da bayray*
Have you ever been to Britain?	**È mai stato in Gran Bretagna?** *e ma-ee stahto een gran braytan-ya*
Did you like it there?	**Le è piaciuto?** *lay e pee-a-chooto*
What part of Italy are you from?	**Da quale parte dell'Italia viene?** *dah kwahlay partay del-leetal-ya vee-e-nay*

CONVERSION CHARTS

In the weight and length charts, the middle figure can be either metric or imperial. Thus 3.3 feet = 1 metre, 1 foot = 0.3 metres, and so on.

feet		metres	inches		cm	lbs		kg
3.3	1	0.3	0.39	1	2.54	2.2	1	0.45
6.6	2	0.61	0.79	2	5.08	4.4	2	0.91
9.9	3	0.91	1.18	3	7.62	6.6	3	1.4
13.1	4	1.22	1.57	4	10.6	8.8	4	1.8
16.4	5	1.52	1.97	5	12.7	11	5	2.2
19.7	6	1.83	2.36	6	15.2	13.2	6	2.7
23	7	2.13	2.76	7	17.8	15.4	7	3.2
26.2	8	2.44	3.15	8	20.3	17.6	8	3.6
29.5	9	2.74	3.54	9	22.9	19.8	9	4.1
32.9	10	3.05	3.9	10	25.4	22	10	4.5
			4.3	11	27.9			
			4.7	12	30.1			

°C	0	5	10	15	17	20	22	24	26	28	30	35	37	38	40	50	100
°F	32	41	50	59	63	68	72	75	79	82	86	95	98.4	100	104	122	212

Km	10	20	30	40	50	60	70	80	90	100	110	120
Miles	6.2	12.4	18.6	24.9	31	37.3	43.5	49.7	56	62	68.3	74.6

Tyre pressures

lb/sq in	15	18	20	22	24	26	28	30	33	35
kg/sq cm	1.1	1.3	1.4	1.5	1.7	1.8	2	2.1	2.3	2.5

Liquids

gallons	1.1	2.2	3.3	4.4	5.5		pints	0.44	0.88	1.76
litres	5	10	15	20	25		litres	0.25	0.5	1

CUSTOMS & PASSPORTS

Streetwise

Visas are not required by visitors from Britain or from the USA, Canada, Australia or New Zealand. Standard EU customs allowances apply in Italy.

I have nothing to declare	**Non ho niente da dichiarare** *nohn o nee-**en**tay da deek-ya-**rah**ray*
I have the usual allowances of alcohol/tobacco	**Ho la quantità consentita di alcool/ tabacco** *o la kwantee-**ta** konsayn-**tee**ta dee alko-**ol**/ ta**bak**-ko*
I have two bottles of wine/a bottle of spirits to declare	**Ho due bottiglie di vino/una bottiglia di liquore da dichiarare** *o doo-ay bot-**teel**-yay dee veeno/oona bot-**teel**-ya dee lee-**kwoh**ray da deek-ya-**rah**ray*
My wife/husband and I have a joint passport	**Io e mia moglie/mio marito siamo sullo stesso passaporto** *ee-oh ay mee-a mol-yay/mee-o ma-**ree**to see-**ah**mo sool-lo stays-so pas-sa-**por**to*
The children are on this passport	**I bambini sono su questo passaporto** *ee bam-beenee sohnoh soo kwaysto pas-sa-**por**to*
I shall be staying in this country for three weeks	**Resterò in questo paese per tre settimane** *ray**stay**ro een kwaysto pa-**ay**zay payr tray sayt-tee-**mah**nay*
We are here on holiday	**Siamo qui in vacanza** *see-**ah**mo kwee een va-**kant**sa*
I am here on business	**Sono qui per affari** *sohnoh kwee payr af-**fah**ree*

DATE & CALENDAR

What is the date today?	**Che giorno è oggi?**	*kay jorno eh od-jee*
It's the ...	**È il ...**	*eh eel ...*
1st of March	**primo marzo**	*preemo martso*
2nd of June	**il due giugno**	*eel doo-ay joon-yo*
We will arrive on the 29th of August	**Arriveremo il 29 agosto**	*arree-vay-**raymo** eel ventee-**novay** **a**gos-to*
1984	**millenovecento-ottantaquattro**	*meel laynovay-**chento**-ot-**tanta**-**kwat**-tro*
Monday	**lunedì**	*loonay-**dee***
Tuesday	**martedì**	*martay-**dee***
Wednesday	**mercoledì**	*mayrko-lay**dee***
Thursday	**giovedì**	*jovay-**dee***
Friday	**venerdì**	*vaynayr-**dee***
Saturday	**sabato**	*sa-bato*
Sunday	**domenica**	*domay-neeka*
January	**gennaio**	*jen-**na**-yo*
February	**febbraio**	*feb-**bra**-yo*
March	**marzo**	*martso*
April	**aprile**	*apree-lay*
May	**maggio**	*mad-jo*
June	**giugno**	*joon-yo*
July	**luglio**	*lool-yo*
August	**agosto**	*a**gohs**-to*
September	**settembre**	*set-**tembray***
October	**ottobre**	*ot-**tohbray***
November	**novembre**	*novem-bray*
December	**dicembre**	*deechem-bray*

See also **NUMBERS**

DENTIST

Streetwise

Dentists will treat you free of charge if you have an E111 form from the Department of Social Security.

I need to see the dentist (urgently)	**Devo farmi vedere dal dentista (urgentemente)** *dayvo fahrmee vay-**day**ray dal dayn-**tee**sta (oorjayn-tay-**mayn**tay)*
I have toothache	**Ho mal di denti** *o mal dee dentee*
I've broken a tooth	**Mi sono spezzato un dente** *mee sohnoh spayts-**sah**to oon dentay*
A filling has come out	**Mi è uscita l'otturazione** *mee e oo-**shee**ta lot-toorats-**yoh**nay*
My gums are bleeding/are sore	**Mi esce sangue dalle gengive/Mi fanno male le gengive** *mee eshay sangway dal-lay jayn-**jee**vay/mee fan-no mahlay lay jayn-**jee**vay*
Please give me an injection	**Mi faccia un'iniezione per favore** *mee fat-cha ooneen-yets-**yoh**nay payr fa-**voh**ray*

THE DENTIST MAY SAY:

Devo fare un'estrazione
*dayvo fahray oonay-strats-**yoh**nay*

I shall have to take it out

Le occorre un'otturazione
*lay ok-kohr-ray oonot-toorats-**yoh**nay*

You need a filling

Questo le potrà fare un po' male
*kwaysto lay po**tra** fahray oon po mahlay*

This might hurt a bit

See also **DOCTOR**

Streetwise

To attract someone's attention, you should preface your question with Scusi (Excuse me).

Excuse me, where is the nearest post office?	**Scusi, dov'è l'ufficio postale più vicino?** *skoo-zee doh-**ve** loof-**fee**cho po-**stah**lay pee-oo vee-**chee**no*
How do I get to the airport?	**Come faccio per andare all'aeroporto?** *kohmay fat-cho payr an-**dah**ray al-la-ayro-**por**to*
Can you tell me the way to ...?	**Può indicarmi la strada per ...?** *pwo eendee-**kahr**mee la strahda payr ...?*
Is this the way to the cathedral?	**È questa la strada che va al duomo?** *e kwaysta la strahda kay va al dwomo*
I am looking for the tourist information office	**Sto cercando l'ufficio informazioni turistiche** *sto chayr-**kan**do loof-**fee**cho eenfor-mats-**yoh**nee too-**ree**steekay*
Which road do I take for ...?	**Quale strada devo prendere per ...?** *kwahlay strahda dayvo **pren**-dayray payr ...*
Is this the turning for ...?	**Devo girare qui per ...?** *dayvo joorah ray kwee payr*
How do I get onto the motorway?	**Come faccio per entrare nell'autostrada?** *kohmay fat-cho payr ayn-**trah**ray nayl-lowto-**strah**da*
How long will it take to get there?	**Quanto tempo ci vuole per arrivarci?** *kwanto tempo chee vwolay payr ar-ree-**vahr**chee*

DOCTOR

Streetwise

Medical advice and treatment are available to British and Irish visitors on the same basis as for Italian subjects. In order to make sure you are treated free of charge, you should take with you form E111, issued by the Department of Social Security.

I need a doctor

Ho bisogno di un medico
*o bee**zohn**-yo dee oon **me**-deeko*

Can I make an appointment with the doctor?

Posso avere un appuntamento con il medico?
*pos-so a-**vay**ray oon ap-poonta-**mayn**to kohn eel **me**-deeko*

My wife is ill

Mia moglie sta male
mee-a mol-yay sta mahlay

I have a sore throat/ a stomach upset

Ho mal di gola/dei disturbi allo stomaco
*o mal dee gohla/day-ee dee-**stoor**bee al-lo **sto**-mako*

He has diarrhoea/ earache

Ha la diarrea/il mal d'orecchio
*a la dee-ar-**ray**-a/eel mal do**rek**-yo*

I am constipated

Sono stitico
*sohnoh **stee**-teeko*

I have a pain here/in my chest

Ho un dolore qui/al petto
*o oon doh-**loh**ray kwee/al pet-to*

He has been stung/bitten

È stato punto/morso
e stahto poonto/morso

He can't breathe/ walk

Non può respirare/camminare
*nohn pwo rayspee-**rah**ray/kam-mee-**nah**ray*

I feel dizzy/sick

Ho il capogiro/la nausea
*o eel kapo-**jee**ro/la **na-oo**zay-a*

I can't sleep/ swallow	**Non riesco a dormire/ad inghiottire** *nohn ree-esko a dor-**mee**ray/ad eeng-yot-**tee**ray*
She has been sick	**Ha vomitato** *a vomee-**tah**to*
I am diabetic/ pregnant	**Sono diabetico/incinta** *sohnoh dee-a-**be**-teeko/een-**cheen**ta*
I am allergic to penicillin/cortisone	**Sono allergico alla penicillina/al cortisone** *sohnoh al-**layr**geeko al-la paynee-cheel-**lee**na/ al kortee-**zoh**nay*
I have high blood pressure	**Ho la pressione alta** *o la prays-**yoh**nay alta*
My blood group is A positive/O negative	**Il mio gruppo sanguigno è A positivo/O negativo** *eel mee o groop po san**gween**-yo e a pozee-**tee**vo/o nayga-**tee**vo*

THE DOCTOR MAY SAY.

Deve restare a letto *dayvay ray-**stah**ray a let-to*	You must stay in bed
Deve andare in ospedale *dayvay an-**dah**ray een ospay-**dah**lay*	You will have to go to hospital
Dovrà subire un intervento *dovra soo-**bee**ray oon eentayr-**vayn**to*	You will need an operation
Prenda questo tre volte al giorno *prenda kwaysto tray voltay al jorno*	Take this three times a day

DRINKS

Streetwise

In larger bars you may have to obtain a receipt (uno scontrino) at the
cash desk (la cassa) before ordering your drink/snack. If you ask for a
coffee (un caffè) you will almost certainly receive an espresso, which
is black and strong and served in a small cup. If you want an espresso
with a dash of milk, ask for un caffè macchiato. A cappuccino is
coffee with milk (which has had steam forced through it to produce a
froth) topped with a sprinkling of chocolate. If you prefer a plain
white coffee, ask for un caffellatte.

A black/white coffee, please	**Un caffè/un cappuccino per favore** *oon kaf-fe/oon kap-poot-cheeno payr fa-vohray*
Two cups of tea	**Due tazze di tè** *doo-ay tat-say dee te*
A pot of tea	**Un tè per due** *oon te payr doo-ay*
A glass of lemonade	**Un bicchiere di limonata** *oon beek-ye-ray dee leemo-nahta*
A bottle of mineral water	**Una bottiglia di acqua minerale** *oona bot-teel-ya dee akwa meenay-rahlay*
Do you have ...?	**Avete ...?** *a-vaytay ..*
Another coffee, please	**Un altro caffè per favore** *oon altro kaf-fe payr fa-vohray*
A draught beer	**Una birra alla spina** *oona beer-ra al-la speena*
With ice, please	**Con ghiaccio per favore** *kohn gee-at-cho payr fa-vohray*

See also **WINES & SPIRITS**

Streetwise

Remember to keep to the right-hand side of the road and that traffic from the right has priority unless otherwise indicated. On three-lane roads the middle lane is for overtaking only and clear indications must be given before making use of that lane. Speed limits are: 50 km/h in built-up areas, 90 km/h outside urban areas where there is no other limit; 110 km/h on dual carriageways and 130 km/h on motorways.

What is the speed limit on this road?	**Qual'è il limite di velocità su questa strada?** *kwal-le eel lee-meetay dee vaylo cheeta soo kwaysta strahda*
Is there a toll on this motorway?	**C'è da pagare il pedaggio su questa autostrada?** *che da pa-gahray eel paydad-jo soo kwaysta owto-strahda*
Is there a short-cut?	**C'è una scorciatoia?** *che oona skorcha-to-ya*
Where can I park?	**Dove posso parcheggiare?** *dohvay pos-so parkayd-jahray*
Is there a car park nearby?	**C'è un parcheggio qui vicino?** *che oon par-ked-jo kwee vee-cheeno*
Can I park here?	**Posso parcheggiare qui?** *pos-so parkayd-jahray kwee*
How long can I stay here?	**Quanto tempo posso restare qui?** *kwanto tempo pos-so rays-tahray kwee*
Do I need a parking disc?	**È necessario il disco orario?** *e nechays-sahr-yo eel deesko orar-yo*

EATING OUT

Streetwise

Trattorie offer excellent food at lower prices than ristoranti, and set-price menus are often good value. Pizzerie (pizza restaurants) and rosticcerie (shops selling roast meat and vegetables to take away or eat on the premises) are also good places for cheaper meals or snacks. Self-service restaurants and fast-food outlets are common now in larger towns, especially tourist centres. You are required by law to obtain a receipt before leaving a restaurant.

Is there a restaurant/ café near here?

C'è un ristorante/un caffè qui vicino?
che oon reesto-rantay/oon kaf-fe kwee vee-cheeno

We want to find somewhere cheap for lunch

Vogliamo pranzare in un posto poco costoso
vol-yahmo prant-sahray een oon pohstoh poko koh-stohzoh

A table for four, please

Un tavolo per quattro per favore
oon tah-volo payr kwat-tro payr fa-vohray

May we see the menu?

Possiamo vedere il menù?
pos-yahmo vay-dayray eel maynoo

We'd like a drink first

Prima prendiamo qualcosa da bere
preema prend-yahmo kwalkoza da bayray

Could we have some more water?

Possiamo avere altra acqua?
pos-yahmo a-vayray altra akwa

We'd like a dessert/ some mineral water

Vorremmo un dolce/dell'acqua minerale
vor-raym-mo oon dohlchay/del-lakwa meenay-rahlay

Is service included?

Il servizio è compreso nel prezzo?
eel sayr-veetsyo e kom-prayzo nayl prets-so

See also **DRINKS, ORDERING, PAYING, WINES & SPIRITS**

Streetwise

Dial 113 for police, ambulance or fire brigade.

There's a fire!	**C'è un incendio!** *che oon een-**chend**-yo*
Call a doctor/an ambulance!	**Chiamate un dottore/un'ambulanza!** *kee-a **mah**tay oon doht-**toh**ray/oon amboo-**lant**sa*
We must get him to hospital	**Dobbiamo portarlo all'ospedale** *dob-**yah**mo por **tar**lo al-lospay-**dah**lay*
Fetch help quickly!	**Andate a chiedere aiuto, presto!** *an-**dah**tay a kee-**e**-dayray a-**yoo**to presto*
Get the police!	**Chiamate la polizia!** *kee-a-**mah**tay la poleet-**see**-a*
Where's the nearest police station/ hospital?	**Dov'è il posto di polizia/ospedale più vicino?** *dohve eel pohstoh dee poleet-**see**-a/ ospay-**dah**lay pee-oo vee-**chee**no*
I've lost my credit card	**Ho perso la mia carta di credito** *o payrso la mee-a karta dee **kray**-deeto*
My child/My handbag is missing	**Ho perso mio figlio/la mia borsa** *o payrso mee-o feel-yo/la mee-a borsa*
My passport/My watch has been stolen	**Mi hanno rubato il passaporto/l'orologio** *mee an-no roo-**bah**to eel pas-sa-**por**to/ lohroh-**lo**joh*
I've forgotten my ticket/my key	**Ho dimenticato il biglietto/le chiavi** *o deemayn-tee-**kah**to eel beel-**yayt**-to/lay kee-**a**vee*

See also **ACCIDENTS, BREAKDOWNS, DENTIST, DOCTOR**

Almost all foreign films shown in Italian cinemas are dubbed, so don't make the mistake of assuming that an English film will be in English with Italian subtitles.

Are there any
local festivals?

Ci sono delle feste locali?
chee sohnoh dayl-lay festay lo-kahlee

Can you recommend
something for the
children?

Può suggerire qualcosa per i bambini?
*pwo sood-jay-reeray kwal-koza payr ee
bam-beenee*

What is there to do
in the evenings?

Che cosa si può fare di sera?
kay koza see pwo fahray dee sayra

Where is there a
cinema/theatre?

Dov'è un cinema/teatro?
dohve oon chee-nayma/tay-atro

Where can we go to
a concert?

Dove possiamo andare per un concerto?
*dohvay pos-yahmo an-dahray payr oon
kon-chayrto*

Can you book the
tickets for us?

Può prenotarci i biglietti?
pwo prayno-tahrchee ee beel-yayt-tee

Is there a swimming
pool?

C'è una piscina?
che oona pee-sheena

Do you know any
interesting walks?

Ci sono delle belle passeggiate da fare?
*chee sohnoh dayl-lay bel-lay pas-sayd-jahtay
da fahray*

Where can we play
tennis/golf?

Dove possiamo giocare a tennis/a golf?
dohvay pos-yahmo jo-kahray a tennis/a golf

See also **NIGHTLIFE, SIGHTSEEING, SPORTS**

What time is the next sailing?	**Quando parte la prossima nave?** *kwando partay la **pros**-seema nahvay*
A return ticket for one car, two adults and two children	**Un biglietto di andata e ritorno per una macchina, due adulti e due bambini** *oon beel-**yayt**-to dee an-**dah**ta ay ree-**tor**no payr oona **mak**-keena doo-ay a-**dool**tee ay doo-ay bam-**bee**-nee*
How long does the crossing take?	**Quanto dura la traversata?** *kwanto doora la-travayr-**sah**ta*
Are there any cabins/ reclining seats?	**Ci sono delle cabine/poltrone reclinabili?** *chee sohnoh dayl-lay ka-**bee**nay/pol-**troh**nay rayklee-**nah**-beelee*
Is there a TV lounge/ bar?	**C'è una sala TV/un bar?** *che oona sahla teevoo/oon bar*
Where are the toilets?	**Dov'è la toilette?** *dohve la twa**let***
Where is the duty-free shop?	**Dov'è il duty-free?** *dohve eel duty free*
Can we go out on deck?	**Possiamo andare sul ponte?** *pos-**yah**mo an **dah**ray sool pohntay*
What is the sea like today?	**Com'è il mare oggi?** *koh**me** eel mahray od-jee*

GIFTS & SOUVENIRS

Where can we buy souvenirs of the cathedral?	**Dove si possono comprare souvenir sul duomo?** *dohvay see **pos**-sono kom-**prah**ray soov-**neer** sool dwomo*
Where is the nearest gift shop?	**Dov'è il negozio di articoli da regalo più vicino?** *dohve eel nay**gots**-yo dee ahr**tee**-kolee da ray-**gah**lo pee-oo vee-**chee**no*
I want to buy a present for my husband/my wife	**Voglio comprare un regalo per mio marito/mia moglie** *vol-yo kom-**prah**ray oon ray-**gah**lo payr mee-oo ma-**ree**to/mee-a mol-yay*
What is the local/regional speciality?	**Quali sono le specialità locali/regionali?** *kwahlee sohnoh lay spaycha-lee**ta** lo-**kah**lee/rayjo-**nah**lee*
Is this hand-made?	**È fatto a mano?** *e fahto a mahno*
Have you anything suitable for a young child?	**Avete qualcosa che vada bene per un bambino piccolo?** *a-**vay**tay kwal-**ko**za kay vahda benay payr oon bam-**bee**no **peek**-kolo*
I want something cheaper/more expensive	**Voglio qualcosa (di) più economico/costoso** *vol-yo kwal-**ko**za (dee) pee-oo ayko-**no**-meeko/kohs-**toh**zoh*
Will this cheese/wine travel well?	**Questo formaggio/vino si conserverà bene in viaggio?** *kwaysto for**mad**-jo/veeno see konsayr-vay**ra** benay een vee-ad-**jo***

In Italian, all nouns are either *masculine* or *feminine*. Where in English we say 'the apple' and 'the book', in Italian it is *la* mela and *il* libro because *mela* is feminine and *libro* is masculine. The gender of nouns is shown in the 'article' (= words for 'the' and 'a') used before them:

Words for 'the':

masc. sing.	**il**	*fem. sing.*	**la**
	l' (+vowel)		**l'** (+vowel)
	lo (+z, gn, pn, ps, x, s+consonant)		
masc. plur.	**i**	*fem. plur.*	**le**
	gli (+vowel, +z, gn, pn, etc)		

Words for 'a':

masculine	**un**	*feminine*	**una**
	uno (+z, gn, pn etc)		**un'** (+vowel)

NOTE: When used after the words **a** (*to, at*), **da** (*by, from*), **su** (*on*), **di** (*of*), and **in** (*in, into*), the words for 'the' contract as follows:

a+il	= al	da+il	= dal	su+il	= sul
a+lo	= allo	da+lo	= dallo	su+lo	= sullo
a+l'	= all'	da+l'	= dall'	su+l'	= sull'
a+la	= alla	da+la	= dalla	su+la	= sulla
a+i	= ai	da+i	= dai	su+i	= sui
a+gli	= agli	da+gli	= dagli	su+gli	= sugli
a+le	= alle	da+le	= dalle	su+le	= sulle

di+il	= del		in+il	= nel
di+lo	= dello		in+lo	= nello
di+l'	= dell'		in+l'	= nell'
di+la	= della		in+la	= nella
di+i	= dei		in+i	= nei
di+gli	= degli		in+gli	= negli
di+le	= delle		in+le	= nelle

e.g. **alla casa** (to the house)
sul tavolo (on the table)

Nouns: formation of plurals

For most nouns, the singular ending changes as follows:

masc. sing.	*masc. plur.*	*example*
o	-i	libr**o** - libr**i**
e	-i	padr**e** - padr**i**
a	-i	artist**a** - artist**i**

NOTE: Most nouns ending in **-co/-go** become **-chi/-ghi** in the plural; nouns ending in **-ca/-ga** become **-chi/-ghi**.

fem. sing.	*fem. plur.*	*example*
a	-e	mel**a** - mel**e**
e	-i	madr**e** - madr**i**

NOTE: Nouns ending in **-ca/-ga** become **-che/-ghe** in the plural; **-cia/-gia** often becomes **-ce/-ge**.

Adjectives

Adjectives normally *follow* the noun they describe in Italian, e.g. la mela **rossa** (*the red apple*).

Some common exceptions which precede the noun are:
bello *beautiful*, **breve** *short*, **brutto** *ugly*, **buono** *good*, **cattivo** *bad*, **giovane** *young*, **grande** *big*, **lungo** *long*, **nuovo** *new*, **piccolo** *small*, **vecchio** *old*.

Italian adjectives have to reflect the gender of the noun they describe. To make an adjective **feminine**, an **-a** replaces the **-o** of the masculine e.g. **rosso** —> **rossa**. Adjectives ending in -e e.g. **giovane**, can be either masculine or feminine. The plural forms of the adjective change in the way described for nouns (above).

'My', 'Your', 'His', 'Her'

These words also depend on the gender and number of the following noun and *not* on the sex of the 'owner'.

	with masc. sing. noun	with fem. sing. noun	with masc. plur. noun	with fem. plur. noun
my	**il mio**	**la mia**	**i miei**	**le mie**
your (: polite)	**il suo**	**la sua**	**i suoi**	**le sue**
(: plural)	**il vostro**	**la vostra**	**i vostri**	**le vostre**
his/her	**il suo**	**la sua**	**i suoi**	**le sue**

GRAMMAR 4

Pronouns

SUBJECT

I	**io**	*ee-o*
you	**lei**	*lay-ee*
he	**lui/egli**	*loo-ee/el-yee*
she	**lei/ella**	*le-ee/el-la*
it (masc.)	**esso**	*es-so*
(fem.)	**essa**	*es-sa*
we	**noi**	*no-ee*
you	**voi**	*vo-ee*
they	**loro**	*lohro*
(things: masc)	**essi**	*es-see*
(: fem)	**esse**	*es-say*

OBJECT

me	**mi**	*mee*
you	**la**	*la*
him	**lo/l'** (+vowel)	*loh/l'*
her	**la/l'** (+vowel)	*la/l'*
it (masc.)	**lo/l'** (+vowel)	*loh, l'*
(fem.)	**la/l'** (+vowel)	*la, l'*
us	**ci**	*chee*
you	**vi**	*vee*
them (masc.)	**li**	*lee*
(fem.)	**le**	*lay*

NOTES:

1. The subject pronouns are often omitted before verbs, since the verb ending generally distinguishes the person:

    vado ...
    I am going ...

2. **Lei** is the polite form for 'you'; **voi** is the plural form.

3. The object pronouns shown above are used to mean *to me, to us* etc, except:

to him/it	= **gli**
to her/it; to you	= **le**
to them	= **loro**

4. Pronoun objects (other than **loro**) usually precede the verb:

lo vedo	BUT:	**scriverò loro**
I see him		I will write to them

    Used with an infinitive (= the verb form given in the dictionary), however, the pronoun follows and is attached to the infinitive minus its final **'e'**:

    voglio comprarlo
    I want to buy it

Verbs

There are three main patterns of endings for verbs in Italian -
those ending **-are**, **-ere** and **-ire** in the dictionary. Two examples
of the **-ire** verbs are shown, since two distinct groups of endings
exist. Subject pronouns are shown in brackets because these are
often not used (see p.45):

	parlare	to speak	**vendere**	to sell
(io)	**parlo**	I speak	**vendo**	I sell
(lei)	**parla**	you speak	**vende**	you sell
(lui/lei)	**parla**	he/she speaks	**vende**	he/she sells
(noi)	**parliamo**	we speak	**vendiamo**	we sell
(voi)	**parlate**	you speak	**vendete**	you sell
(loro)	**parlano**	they speak	**vendono**	they sell

	dormire	to sleep	**finire**	to finish
(io)	**dormo**	I sleep	**finisco**	I finish
(lei)	**dorme**	you sleep	**finisce**	you finish
(lui/lei)	**dorme**	he/she sleeps	**finisce**	he/she finishes
(noi)	**dormiamo**	we sleep	**finiamo**	we finish
(voi)	**dormite**	you sleep	**finite**	you finish
(loro)	**dormono**	they sleep	**finiscono**	they finish

And in the past:

(io)	**ho parlato**	I spoke	**ho venduto**	I sold
(lei)	**ha parlato**	you spoke	**ha venduto**	you sold
(lui/lei)	**ha parlato**	he/she spoke	**ha venduto**	she sold
(noi)	**abbiamo parlato**	we spoke	**abbiamo venduto**	we sold
(voi)	**avete parlato**	you spoke	**avete venduto**	you sold
(loro)	**hanno parlato**	they spoke	**hanno venduto**	they sold

(io)	**ho dormito**	I slept	**ho finito**	I finished
(lei)	**ha dormito**	you slept	**ha finito**	you finished
(lui/lei)	**ha dormito**	she slept	**ha finito**	he/she finished
(noi)	**abbiamo dormito**	we slept	**abbiamo finito**	we finished
(voi)	**avete dormito**	you slept	**avete finito**	you finished
(loro)	**hanno dormito**	they slept	**hanno finito**	they finished

Among the most important *irregular* verbs are the following:

	essere	to be	**avere**	to have
(io)	**sono**	I am	**ho**	I have
(lei)	**è**	you are	**ha**	you have
(lui/lei)	**è**	he/she is	**ha**	he/she has
(noi)	**siamo**	we are	**abbiamo**	we have
(voi)	**siete**	you are	**avete**	you have
(loro)	**sono**	they are	**hanno**	they have

	andare	to go	**fare**	to do
(io)	**vado**	I go	**faccio**	I do
(lei)	**va**	you go	**fa**	you do
(lui/lei)	**va**	he/she goes	**fa**	he/she does
(noi)	**andiamo**	we go	**facciamo**	we do
(voi)	**andate**	you go	**fate**	you do
(loro)	**vanno**	they go	**fanno**	they do

GREETINGS

Streetwise

Remember that familiar forms are only used when you know someone well or are invited to do so. Otherwise use the formal forms. Similarly, Ciao (hello) is only used to greet people you are on familiar terms with. The words Signore, Signora, and Signorina are used far more frequently than 'Sir' or 'Madam' are used in English. Thus, in hotels you are likely to be greeted with 'Buon giorno Signore' etc. Likewise, you should say 'Buona sera Signore' to an official rather than simply 'Buona sera'.

Hello	**Buon giorno** *bwon jorno*
Good morning/Good afternoon/Good evening	**Buon giorno/Buona sera/Buona sera** *bwon jorno/bwona sayra/bwona sayra*
Goodbye	**Arrivederci** *ar-reevay-**dayr**chee*
Good night	**Buona notte** *bwona not-tay*
How do you do?	**Piacere!** *pee-a-**chay**ray*
Pleased to meet you	**Piacere di conoscerla** *pee-a-**chay**ray dee ko-**no**-shayrla*
How are you?	**Come sta?** *kohmay sta*
Fine, thank you	**Bene grazie** *benay grats-yay*
See you soon	**A presto** *a presto*

See also **GRAMMAR**

I'd like to make an appointment	**Vorrei prendere un appuntamento** *vor-**re**-ee **pren**-dayray oon ap-poonta-**mayn**to*
A cut and blow-dry, please	**Vorrei tagliare i capelli e fare la messa in piega con il föhn** *vor-**re**-ee tal-**yah**ray ee ka**payl**-lee ay fahray la mays-sa een pee-e-ga kohn eel fon*
A shampoo and set	**Vorrei fare la messa in piega** *vor-**re**-ee fahray la mays-sa een pee-e-ga*
Not too short	**Non troppo corti** *nohn trop-po kortee*
I'd like it layered	**Mi piacciono scalati** *mee pee-**at**-chono ska-**lah**tee*
Take more off the top/the sides	**Tagli di più sopra/ai lati** *talyee dee pee-oo sohpra/a-ee lahtee*
My hair is permed/tinted	**I miei capelli hanno la permanente/sono tinti** *ee mee-e-ee ka**payl**-lee an no la payrma-**nen**tay/sohnoh teentee*
My hair is naturally curly/straight	**I miei capelli sono mossi/dritti al naturale** *ee mee-e-ee ka**payl**-lee sohnoh mos see/dreet tee al natôo **rah**lay*
It's too hot	**È troppo caldo** *e trop-poh kaldo*
I'd like a conditioner, please	**Vorrei un balsamo per favore** *vor-**re**-ee oon **bal**-samo payr fa-**voh**ray*

HOTEL DESK

Streetwise

On arrival at your hotel you will usually be asked to hand over your passport(s) ('i documenti, per favore'). This is to allow the hotel management to register your name(s) with the police. By law, all tourists must register with the police within three days of entering Italy. It is up to the tourist to check that it has been done. Once registered, you are permitted to stay in Italy as a tourist for up to three months.

I have reserved a room in the name of ...	**Ho prenotato una stanza a nome di ...** *o prayno-**tah**to oona stantsa a nohmay dee ...*
I confirmed my booking by phone/by letter	**Ho confermato la prenotazione con una telefonata/lettera** *o konfayr-**mah**to la prayno-tats-**yoh**nay kohn oona taylay-fo-**nah**ta/**let**-tayra*
What time is breakfast/dinner?	**A che ora è la colazione/la cena?** *a kay ohra e la kolats-**yoh**nay/la chayna*
Can we have breakfast in our room at ... o'clock?	**Ci può portare la colazione nella nostra stanza alle ...?** (*see* TIME) *chee pwo por-**tah**ray la kolats-**yoh**nay nel-la nostra stantsa al-lay ...*
Please call me at ...	**Per favore chiamatemi alle ...** (*see* TIME) *payr fa-**voh**ray kee-a-**mah**-taymee al-lay...*
Can I have my key?	**Posso avere la mia chiave?** *pos-so a-**vay**ray la mee-a kee-**ah**vay*
Do you have any messages for me?	**Avete qualche messaggio per me?** *a-**vay**tay kwalkay may**sad**-jo payr may*
I shall be leaving at ... tomorrow morning	**Partirò domani mattina alle ...** (*see* TIME) *pahrtee-**ro** do-**mah**nee mat-**tee**na al-lay ...*

See also **ACCOMMODATION, PAYING, ROOM SERVICE**

Streetwise

At most railway stations you can leave your luggage at the left-luggage office for a small fee. Look for the sign deposito bagagli. Luggage can also be sent from main-line Italian stations to principal European stations and vice versa. Enquire at the same office.

Where do I check-in my luggage?
Dove posso consegnare i bagagli?
dohvay pos-so konsaynyahray ee bagal-yee

Where is the luggage from the London flight/train?
Dove sono i bagagli del volo/treno da Londra?
dohvay sohnoh ee bagal-yee dayl vohloh/treno da lohndra

Our luggage has not arrived
I nostri bagagli non sono arrivati
ee nostree ba-gal-yee nohn sohnoh ar ree-vahtee

My suitcase was damaged in transit
La mia valigia è stata danneggiata durante il viaggio
la mee-a va-leeja e stahta dan-nayd-jahta doo-rantay eel vee-ad-jo

Where is the left luggage office?
Dov'è il deposito bagagli?
dohve eel daypo-zeeto bagal-yee

Are there any luggage trolleys?
Ci sono dei carrelli per i bagagli?
chee sohnoh day-ee kar-rel-lee payr ee bagal-yee

Can you help me with my bags, please?
Può aiutarmi a portare le valigie per favore?
pwo a-yoo-tahrmee a por-tahray lay va-leejay payr fa-vohray

Please take my bags to a taxi
Per favore porti le mie valigie al taxi
payr fa-vohray portee lay mee-ay va-leejay al taxee

MAPS & GUIDES

Streetwise

Tourist offices and some hotels will provide free maps of the town or resort you are staying in. Ask for una piantina (street plan) or una carta (map).

Where can I buy a local map?
Dove posso comprare una cartina?
dohvay pos-so kom-prahray oona kahr-teena

Have you got a town plan?
Avete una piantina della città?
a-vaytay oona pee-an-teena dayl-la cheet-ta

I want a street map of the city
Voglio una piantina della città
vol-yo oon pee-an-teena dayl-la cheet-ta

I need a road map of ...
Ho bisogno di una carta stradale di ...
o beezohn-yo dee oona kahrta stra-dahlay dee ...

Can I get a map at the tourist office?
Posso prendere una cartina all'ufficio informazioni turistiche?
pos-so pren-dayray oona kahr-teena al-loo-feecho eenform-mats-yohnee tooree-steekay

Can you show me on the map?
Può mostrarmelo sulla cartina?
pwo mostrahr-melo sool-la kahr-teena

Do you have a guidebook in English?
Avete una guida in inglese?
a-vaytay oona gweeda een een-glayzay

Do you have a guidebook to the cathedral?
Avete una guida sulla cattedrale?
a-vaytay oona gweeda sool-la kat-taydrahlay

I need an English-Italian dictionary
Ho bisogno di un dizionario inglese-italiano
o beezohn-yo dee oon deets-yo-nar-yo een-glayzay eetal-yahno

See also **DIRECTIONS**

MEASUREMENTS

a pint of ...
un mezzo litro di ...
oon medz-zo leetro dee

a litre of ...
un litro di ...
oon leetro dee

a kilo of ...
un kilo di ...
oon keelo dee

a pound of ...
un mezzo kilo di ...
oon medz-zo keelo dee

100 grammes of ...
un etto di ...
oon et-to dee

half a kilo of ...
un mezzo kilo di ...
oon medz-zo keelo dee

a half-bottle of ...
un mezzo litro di ...
oon medz-zo leetro dee

a slice of ...
una fetta di
oona fayt-ta dee

a portion of ...
una porzione di ...
oona portsee-oh-nay dee

a dozen ...
una dozzina di ...
oona dodz-zeena dee

1500 lira's worth
1500 lire di ...
meel-lay-cheen-kway-chento leeray dee

a third
un terzo
oon tayrtso

two thirds
due terzi
doo-ay tayrtsee

a quarter
un quarto
oon kwarto

three quarters
tre quarti
tray kwartee

ten per cent
il dieci per cento
eel dee-e-chee payr chento

more of
più di
pee-oo dee

less of
meno di
mayno dee

enough of
abbastanza
ab-ba-stantsa

double
il doppio
eel dop-pee-o

twice
due volte
dooay voltay

three times
tre volte
tray voltay

See also **BUYING, CONVERSION CHARTS, NUMBERS, PAYING**

Italians generally eat three main meals per day:

- *la (prima) colazione*, a light breakfast often consisting of only *caffellatte* (white coffee) with bread, butter and jam, or the famous *cappuccino e cornetto* (cappuccino and cake) that many people take at a bar on the way to work.
- *il pranzo* or *la seconda colazione* (lunch), eaten between mid-day and two o'clock. For many Italians this is the main meal of the day (hence the famous *siesta*).
- *la cena* (dinner) is normally eaten after 7.30 p.m.

Generally the courses on a menu will be as follows for both lunch and dinner:

Antipasti - hors d'oeuvre/starters
Primi Piatti - first course (normally pasta or risotto)
Secondi Piatti - second/main course (meat, fish or poultry)
Contorni - side-dishes (vegetables: peas, beans, spinach, etc)
Formaggi - cheeses
Dolci - desserts
Frutta di Stagione - fresh fruit
Caffè - coffee

Note that the *menù turistico* (tourist menu) or the *menù a prezzo fisso* (fixed-price menu) often represent good value for money.

How is this dish served?	**Come servite questo piatto?** *kohmay sayr-veetay kwesto peeat-to*
What is the house speciality?	**Qual'è la specialità della casa?** *kwahle la spaycha-leeta dayl-la kasa*
What kind of pasta/seafood/vegetables do you have?	**Che tipo di pasta/frutti di mare/verdura avete?** *kay teepo dee pasta/froot-tee dee mahray/vayr-doora a-vaytay*

    See also **EATING OUT, ORDERING, WINES & SPIRITS**

Streetwise

The unit of currency is the Italian lira (plural lire). Banks are open from 0830-1320 Mon.-Fri., and some are also open from 1500-1600 Mon.-Fri. Many hotels will cash traveller's cheques and both cheques and cash can also be exchanged at the bureaux de change (cambio) at airports and railway stations. If exchanging money in a private bureau, check how much commission is being charged. Wherever you change your money, you will need to show your passport

I haven't enough money	**Non ho abbastanza soldi** *nohn o ab-ba-**stan**tsa soldee*
Have you any change?	**Avete da cambiare?** *a-**vay**tay da kamb-**yah**ray*
Can you change a 50,000 lire note?	**Può cambiare un biglietto da 50.000 lire?** *pwo kamb **yah**ray oon beel-**yayt**-to da cheenkwan-ta-**mee**la leeray*
I'd like to change these traveller's cheques	**Vorrei cambiare questi traveller's cheque** *vor-**re**-ee kamb-**yah**ray kwaystee travellers cheque*
I want to change some lire into pounds	**Vorrei cambiare queste lire in sterline** *vor-**re**-ee kamb-**yah**ray kwaystay leeray een stayr-**lee**nay*
What is the rate for sterling?	**Qual'è il cambio per la sterlina?** *kwahle eel kamb-yo payr la stayr-**lee**na*
Can I get a cash advance with my credit card?	**Posso avere un anticipo con la mia carta di credito?** *pos-so a-**vay**ray oon an**tee**-cheepo kohn la mee-a karta dee **kray**-deeto*
How do I get reimbursed?	**Come si fa per essere rimborsati?** *kohmay see fa payr es-sayray reembor-**sah**tee*

NIGHTLIFE

Streetwise

Note that ticket prices at discos and night clubs normally include the cost of your first drink.

What is there to do in the evenings?	**Che cosa si può fare di sera?** *kay koza see pwo fahray dee sayra*
Where can we go to see a cabaret/go to dance?	**Dove possiamo andare per vedere un cabaret/per ballare?** *dohvay pos-yahmo an-dahray payr vay-dayray oon kaba-re/payr bal-lahray*
Are there any good night clubs/discos?	**Ci sono dei buoni locali notturni/delle buone discoteche?** *chee sohnoh day-ee bwonee lo-kahlee not-toornee/dayl-lay bwonay deesko-tekay*
How do we get to the casino?	**Come ci si arriva al casinò?** *kohmay chee see ar-reeva al kazee-no*
How much does it cost to get in?	**Quanto costa il biglietto di entrata?** *kwanto kohsta eel beel-yayt-to dee ayn-trahta*
We'd like to reserve two seats for tonight	**Vorremmo prenotare due posti per stasera** *vor-raym-mo prayno-tahray doo-ay pohstee payr sta-sayra*
Is there a bar/a restaurant?	**C'è un bar/un ristorante?** *che oon bar/oon reesto-rantay*
What time does the show/concert begin?	**A che ora inizia lo spettacolo/il concerto?** *a kay ohra eeneets-ya loh spayt-tah-kolo/ eel kon-chayrto*

See also EATING OUT, ENTERTAINMENT

0	**zero** *dzero*	13	**tredici** *tray-deechee*	50	**cinquanta** *cheenkwan-ta*
1	**uno, una** *oono, oona*	14	**quattordici** *kwat-tor-deechee*	60	**sessanta** *says-santa*
2	**due** *dooay*	15	**quindici** *kween-deechee*	70	**settanta** *sayt-tanta*
3	**tre** *tray*	16	**sedici** *say-deechee*	80	**ottanta** *oht-tanta*
4	**quattro** *kwat-tro*	17	**diciasette** *deechas-set-tay*	90	**novanta** *noh-vanta*
5	**cinque** *cheen-kway*	18	**diciotto** *deechot-to*	100	**cento** *chento*
6	**sei** *se-ee*	19	**diciannove** *deechan-novay*	110	**cento dieci** *chento dee-e-chee*
7	**sette** *set-te*	20	**venti** *vayntee*	200	**duecento** *doo-ay-chento*
8	**otto** *ot-to*	21	**ventuno** *vayn-toono*	300	**trecento** *tray chento*
9	**nove** *novay*	22	**ventidue** *vayntee-doo-ay*	1,000	**mille** *meel-lay*
10	**dieci** *dee-e-chee*	23	**ventitre** *vayntee-tray*	2,000	**duemila** *doo-ay-meela*
11	**undici** *oon-deechee*	30	**trenta** *trayn-ta*	1,000,000	**un milione** *oon meel-yohnay*
12	**dodici** *doh-deechee*	40	**quaranta** *kwaran-ta*		

1st	**primo** *preemo*	5th	**quinto** *kweento*	9th	**nono** *nonoh*
2nd	**secondo** *saykohn-do*	6th	**sesto** *sesto*	10th	**decimo** *dechee-mo*
3rd	**terzo** *tayrtso*	7th	**settimo** *set-teemo*		
4th	**quarto** *kwarto*	8th	**ottavo** *oht-tahvo*		

See also **MEASUREMENTS**

ORDERING

Streetwise

Many restaurants offer set price menus (menù turistici) which are often good value, although it is wise to compare the price with the individual items on the normal menu. Most restaurants add a cover charge (coperto) as well as a service charge (servizio) of around 10%.

Do you have a set menu/a special menu for children?

Avete un menù fisso/un menù speciale per bambini?
a-vaytay oon maynoo fees-so/oon maynoo spay-chahlay payr bam-beenee

We will have the menu at ... lire

Prendiamo il menù a ... lire (*see* NUMBERS)
prend-yahmo eel maynoo a ... leeray

May we see the wine list?

Possiamo vedere la lista dei vini?
pos-yahmo vay-dayray la leesta day-ee veenee

What do you recommend?

Che cosa ci consiglia?
kay koza chee konseel-ya

Is there a local speciality?

C'è una specialità locale?
che oona spaycha-leeta lo-kahlay

Are the vegetables included?

Comprende anche i contorni?
kom-prenday ankay ee kon-tornee

Rare/medium rare/well done, please

Al sangue/poco cotta/cotta bene, per favore
al sangway/poko kot-ta/kot-ta benay payr fa-vohray

We'd like a dessert/some coffee, please

Vorremmo un dolce/il caffè, per favore
vor-raym-mo oon dohlchay/eel kaf-fe payr fa-vohray

See also COMPLAINTS, EATING OUT, MENUS, WINES & SPIRITS

Streetwise

Major international credit and charge cards are accepted in most large hotels, restaurants and shops. Traveller's cheques and Eurocheques (supported by a valid card) may also be accepted as payment. Remember to pick up the receipt if you make a purchase, or pay for a drink in a bar, etc. It is illegal to leave a bar, shop or restaurant without one. At one time you often received sweets as change due to a shortage of small coins. This is becoming less common.

Can I have the bill, please?	**Mi può portare il conto, per favore?** *mee pwo por-tahray eel kohntoh payr fa-vohray*
Is service/tax included?	**Il servizio è compreso/L'IVA è compresa?** *eel sayrveets-yo e kom-prayzo/leeva e kom-prayza*
What does that come to?	**Quanto fa in tutto?** *kwanto fa een toot-to*
How much is it?	**Quanto costa?** *kwanto kohsta*
Do I pay in advance?	**Pago in anticipo?** *pahgo een antee cheepo*
Do I pay a deposit?	**Devo pagare un acconto?** *dayvo pa-gahray oon ak-kohnto*
Can I pay by cheque?	**Posso pagare con un assegno?** *pos-so pa-gahray kohn oon as-sayn yo*
Do you accept traveller's cheques?	**Accettate i traveller's cheque?** *at-chayt-tahtay ee travellers cheque*
I'd like a receipt, please	**Vorrei una ricevuta, per favore** *vor-re ee oona reechay-voota payr fa-vohray*

PERSONAL DETAILS

My name is ...

Mi chiamo ...
*mee kee-**ahm**o ...*

My date of birth is ...

Sono nato il ...
sohnoh nahto eel ...

My address is ...

Il mio indirizzo è ...
*eel mee-o eendee-**reets**-so e ...*

I come from Britain/America

Vengo dalla Gran Bretagna/dall'America
*vengo dal-la gran bray**tan**-ya/dal-la**may**-reeka*

I live in London/Scotland

Abito a Londra/in Scozia
ah-beeto a lohndra/een skots-ya

My passport/driving licence number is ...

Il numero del mio passaporto/della mia patente è ... (see NUMBERS)
*eel **noo**-mayro dayl mee-o pas-sa-**por**to/dayl-la mee-a pa-**ten**tay e ...*

My blood group is ...

Il mio gruppo sanguigno è ...
*eel mee-o groop-po san**gween**-yo e ...*

I work in an office/a factory

Lavoro in un ufficio/un'industria
*la-**voh**ro een oon oof-**fee**cho/ooneen-**doo**stree-a*

I am a secretary/manager

Sono una segretaria/un direttore
*sohnoh oona saygray-**tar**-ya/oon deerayt-**toh**ray*

I'm here on holiday/business

Sono qui in vacanza/per affari
*sohnoh kwee een va-**kan**tsa/payr af-**fah**ree*

My daughter/son is six

Mia figlia/mio figlio ha sei anni
*mee-a **feel**-ya/mee-o **feel**-yo a se-ee an-nee*

Streetwise

Petrol stations can be found at frequent intervals along main roads and motorways (autostrade). Petrol in Italy is the most expensive in Europe. Unleaded petrol (benzina senza piombo/benzina verde) is widely available, as is diesel (gasolio) and 4-star (super). Pumps are often attended.

20 litres of 4 star	**20 litri di super** *vayntee leetree dee soopayr*
20,000 liras' (worth) of 4 star	**20.000 lire di super per favore** *vayntee-meela leeray dee soopayr payr fa-vohray*
Fill it up, please	**Il pieno, per favore** *eel pee-e-no payr fa-vohray*
Can you check the oil/the water?	**Può controllare l'olio/l'acqua?** *pwo kontrohl-lah-ray lol-yo/lakwa*
Could you clean the windscreen?	**Potrebbe pulire il vetro?** *potreb-bay poo leeray eel vaytro*
Where's the air line?	**Dove posso controllare la pressione delle gomme?** *dohvay pos-so kontrol-lahray la prays-yohnay dayl lay gohm-may*
Can I have a can of petrol/oil?	**Posso avere una lattina di benzina/olio?** *pos-so a-vayray oona lat-teena dee baynd-zeena/ol-yo*
Is there a lavatory?	**C'è un gabinetto?** *che oon gabee-nayt-to*
How do I use the car wash?	**Come funziona il lavaggio auto?** *kohmay foonts-yohna eel lavad-jo owto*

See also **BREAKDOWNS, DRIVING, PAYING**

PHOTOGRAPHY

Streetwise

Chemist's in Italy do not sell photographic equipment or develop films as they do in Britain. Instead you must take your films to a specialist shop dealing in photographic equipment (foto-ottica). Having films developed in Italy can prove expensive.

I need a colour/ black and white film	**Ho bisogno di un rullino a colori/in bianco e nero** *o bee-**zohn**-yo dee oon rool-**lee**no a koh-**loh**ree/ een bee-**an**ko ay nayro*
It is for prints/ slides	**È per fotografie/diapositive** *e payr foto-gra-**fee**-ay/dee-a-pozee-**tee**vay*
The film has jammed	**Il rullino si è bloccato** *eel rool-**lee**no see e blok-**kah**to*
The rewind mechanism does not work	**Il meccanismo di ravvolgimento non funziona** *eel mayk-ka-**neez**mo dee rav-voljee-**mayn**to nohn foonts-**yoh**na*
Can you develop this film, please?	**Può sviluppare questo rullino, per favore?** *pwo zveeloop-**pah**ray kwaysto rool-**lee**no payr fa-**voh**ray*
When will the photos be ready?	**Quando saranno pronte le foto?** *kwando sa**ran**-no prohntay lay fotoh*
Can I take photos in here?	**Posso fare delle foto qui dentro?** *pos-so fahray dayl-lay fotoh kwee dayntro*
Would you take a photo of us, please?	**Può farci una foto, per favore?** *pwo fahrchee oona fotoh payr fa-**voh**ray*

Streetwise

There are various types of police in Italy, each dealing with a different area of the law. The Carabinieri *report to the Ministry of Defence and tend to deal with more serious crimes. The* Polizia *is a civil force which deals with crime and administrative matters (such as lost passports, etc). In towns, traffic is controlled by the* Vigili urbani *who can also deal with less serious criminal offences. Outside the towns, the roads are patrolled by the* Polizia stradale *(traffic police).*

We should call the police	**Dovremmo chiamare la polizia** *dovraym-mo kee-a-mahray la poleet-see-a*
Where is the police station?	**Dov'è il commissariato?** *dohve eel kom-mees-sar-yahto*
My car has been broken into	**Mi hanno aperto la macchina** *mee an-no a-payrto la mak-keena*
I've been robbed	**Sono stato derubato** *sohnoh stahto dayroo-bahto*
I have had an accident	**Ho avuto un incidente** *o a-vooto oon eenchee-dentay*
How much is the fine?	**Quant'è la multa?** *kwan-te la moolta*
How do I pay it?	**Come pago?** *kohmay pago*
I don't have my driving licence on me	**Non ho la patente con me** *nohn o la pa-tentay kohn may*
I'm very sorry, officer	**Mi dispiace molto signor poliziotto** *mee deespee-achay mohltoh seen-yohr poleetz-yot-to*

See also **ACCIDENTS, CUSTOMS & PASSPORTS, EMERGENCIES**

POST OFFICE

Streetwise

Stamps can also be bought at a tabaccheria (tobacconist's). Allow 7 to 10 days for letters to and from Italy. Post offices are indicated by a round yellow sign bearing the letters PT. At larger post offices there may be telephone booths where you can make long-distance calls.

How much is a letter to England/America?	**Quanto costa un francobollo per l'Inghilterra/l'America?** *kwanto kohsta oon franko-**bohl**lo payr leengeel-**ter**-ra/lamày-reeka*
I'd like six stamps for postcards to Germany, please	**Vorrei sei francobolli per cartoline per la Germania, per favore** *vor-**re**-ee se-ee franko-**bohl**lee payr karto-**lee**nay payr la jayr**man**-ya payr fa-**voh**ray*
Twelve …-lira stamps, please	**Dodici francobolli da … lire per favore** *doh-deechee franko-**bohl**lee da … leeray payr fa-**voh**ray*
I want to send a telegram to …	**Voglio mandare un telegramma in ...** *vol-yo man-**dah**ray oon taylay-**gram**-ma een ...*
How much will it cost?	**Quanto potrà costare?** *kwanto po**tra** koh-**stah**ray*
Do I have to fill in a form?	**C'è bisogno di compilare una scheda?** *che bee**zohn**-yo dee kompee-**lah**ray oona skeda*
I want to send this parcel	**Voglio spedire questo pacco** *vol-yo spay-**dee**ray kwaysto pak-ko*
I'd like to make a telephone call	**Vorrei fare una telefonata** *vor-**re**-ee fahray oona taylay-fo-**na**ta*

64

Can you help me, please?	**Può aiutarmi, per favore?** *pwo a-you-**tahr**mee payr fa-**voh**ray*
What is the matter?	**Che cosa c'è?** *kay koza che*
I am in trouble	**Ho bisogno di aiuto** *o bee**zohn**-yo dee a-**yoo**to*
I don't understand	**Non capisco** *nohn ka-**pee**sko*
Do you speak English?	**Parla inglese?** *parla een-**glay**zay*
Please repeat that	**Ripeta per favore** *ree-**pe**-ta payr fa-**voh**ray*
I have run out of money	**Sono rimasto senza soldi** *sohnoh ree-**ma**sto sentsa soldee*
My son is lost	**Non trovo più mio figlio** *nohn trohvoh pee-oo mee-o feel-yo*
I have lost my way	**Mi sono perso** *mee sohnoh payrso*
I have forgotten my passport	**Ho dimenticato il passaporto** *o deemayn-tee-**kah**to eel pas-sa-**por**to*
Where is the British Consulate?	**Dov'è il consolato britannico?** *dohve eel konso-**lah**to breetan-neeko*
Leave me alone!	**Lasciami in pace!** ***lash**-amee een pa-chay*
Go away!	**Va' via!** *va vee-a*

See also **ACCIDENTS, COMPLAINTS, EMERGENCIES, POLICE**

PRONUNCIATION

In the pronunciation system used in this book, Italian sounds are represented by spellings of the nearest possible sounds in English. Hence, when you read out the pronunciation - the line in italics after each phrase or word - sound the letters as if you were reading an English word. Whenever we think it is not sufficiently clear where to stress a word or phrase, we have used **heavy italics** to highlight the syllable to be stressed. The following notes should help you:

	REMARKS	EXAMPLE	PRONUNCIATION
ay	As in day	**dei**	day-ee
ah	As a in father	**prendiamo**	prend-**yah**mo
e	As in bed	**letto**	let-to
oh	As in go, low	**sono**	sohnoh
y	As in yet	**aiuto**	a-**yoo**to
ow	As in cow	**automobile**	owto-**moh**-beelay

Spelling in Italian is very regular and, with a little practice, you will soon be able to pronounce Italian words from their spelling alone. The only letters which may cause problems are:

i	As ee in meet	**vino**	veeno
	or as y in yet	**aiuto**	a-**yoo**to
u	As oo in boot	**luna**	loona
	or as w in will	**buon**	bwon
c	Before e, i as ch in chat	**centro**	chentro
	Before a, o, u as in cat	**cosa**	koza
ch	As c in cat	**chi**	kee
g	Before e, i as in gin	**giorno**	jorno
	Before a, h, o, u as in get	**regalo**	ray-**gah**lo
gl	As lli in million	**figlio**	**feel**-yo
gn	As ni in onion	**bisogno**	bee**zohn**-yo
h	Silent	**ho**	o
sc	Before e, i, as sh in shop	**uscita**	oo-**shee**ta
	Before a, o, u as in scar	**capisco**	ka-**pee**sko
z	As ts in cats	**senza**	sentsa
	or ds in rods	**mezzo**	medz-zo

Streetwise

Many businesses close for part or even the whole of August as most Italians take their holidays then. Ferragosto, 15 August, is one of the most important public holidays and many towns hold parties, firework displays, etc to celebrate it. The sign chiuso per ferie *on a shop or restaurant door or window means 'closed for the holidays'.*

New Year's Day	January 1st
Easter Monday	
Liberation Day	April 25th
Labour Day	May 1st
Assumption	August 15th
All Saints' Day	November 1st
Immaculate Conception	December 8th
Christmas Day	December 25th
St Stephen's Day	December 26th

RAILWAY STATION

Streetwise

Children under twelve pay half fare and those under four travel free. Few trains have snack bars, but at larger stations refreshments and rolls are sold on the platform. At main railway stations you will also find alberghi diurni (day hotels) which offer toilets and fully-equipped bathrooms plus hairdressers, cleaning services and other facilities.

What time are the trains to ...?	**A che ora ci sono i treni per ...?** *a kay ohra chee sohnoh ee trenee payr ...*
When is the next train to ...?	**Quando parte il prossimo treno per ...?** *kwando pahrtay eel **pros**-seemo treno payr ...*
What time does it get there?	**A che ora arriva?** *a kay ohra ar-**reev**a*
Do I have to change?	**Devo cambiare?** *dayvo kamb-**yah**ray*
A single/return to ..., first/second class	**Un biglietto di andata/andata e ritorno per ..., prima/seconda classe** *oon beel-**yayt**-to dee an-**dah**ta/an-**dah**ta ay ree-**tor**no payr ..., preema/say-**kohn**da*
I want to book a seat in a non-smoking compartment	**Voglio prenotare un posto in uno scompartimento non fumatori** *vol-yo prayno-**tah**ray oon pohstoh een oono skompar-tee-**mayn**to nohn fooma-**toh**ree*
I want to reserve a couchette/sleeper	**Voglio prenotare una cuccetta/un posto sul vagone letto** *vol-yo prayno-**tah**ray oona koot-**chet**ta/oon pohstoh sool va-**goh**nay let-to*
Which platform for the train to ...?	**Da che binario parte il treno per ...?** *da kay bee**nar**-yo pahrtay eel treno payr ...*

See also **LUGGAGE, TRAIN TRAVEL**

I have broken the window	**Ho rotto un vetro** *o roht-toh oon vaytro*
There is a hole in these trousers	**C'è un buco in questi pantaloni** *che oon booko een kwaystee panta-**lohn**ee*
This is broken/torn	**Questo è rotto/strappato** *kwaysto e roht-toh/strap-**pah**to*
Can you repair this?	**Può riparare questo?** *pwo reepa **rah**ray kwaysto*
Can you do it quickly?	**Può farlo presto?** *pwo fahrlo presto*
When can you get it done by?	**Quando potrà finirlo?** *kwando potra fee-**neer**lo*
I need some adhesive tape/a safety pin	**Ho bisogno di nastro adesivo/di una spilla di sicurezza** *o bee**zohn**-yo dee nastro aday-**zee**vo/dee oona speel-la dee seekoo **rayts**-sa*
The stitching has come undone	**Si è scucito** *see e skoo-**chee**to*
Can you reheel these shoes?	**Può rifare i tacchi a queste scarpe?** *pwo ree-**fah**ray ee tak-kee a kwaystay skarpay*
The screw has come loose	**La vite si è allentata** *la veetay see e al-layn-**tah**ta*
The handle has come off	**È uscita la maniglia** *e oo-**shee**ta la ma**neel**-ya*

See also **ACCIDENTS, BREAKDOWNS, EMERGENCIES**

ROAD CONDITIONS

Streetwise

The motorway (autostrada) system in Italy is excellent, but remember that you have to pay a toll (pedaggio). (At the entrance to the motorway you are given a ticket showing where you joined the motorway. At the exit you pay according to the distance travelled.) Minor roads are not so well maintained and in the mountains in winter snow-chains may be required.

Is there a route that avoids the traffic?	**C'è un'altra strada per evitare il traffico?** *che oonal-tra strahda payr ayvee-tahray eel **traf**-feeko*
Is the traffic heavy on the motorway?	**C'è molto traffico sull'autostrada?** *che mohltoh **traf**-feeko sool-lowto-**strah**da*
What is causing this hold-up?	**Perché c'è questo ingorgo?** *payr**kay** che kwaysto een-**gor**go*
When will the road be clear?	**Quando sarà libera la strada?** *kwando sa**ra lee**-bayra la strahda*
Is there a detour?	**C'è una deviazione?** *che oona dayvee-ats-**yoh**nay*
Is the road to ... snowed up?	**La strada per ... è bloccata dalla neve?** *la strahda payr ... e blok-**kah**ta dal-la nayvay*
Is the pass/tunnel open?	**È aperto il passo/È aperta la galleria?** *e a-**payr**to eel pas-so/e a-**payr**ta la gal-lay-**ree**-a*
Do I need chains/ studded tyres?	**C'è bisogno di catene/gomme chiodate?** *che bee**zohn**-yo dee ka-**tay**nay/gohm-may kee-o-**dah**tay*

See also **DRIVING**, **WEATHER**

We'd like breakfast/ a bottle of wine in our room	**Vorremmo la colazione/una bottiglia di vino nella nostra camera** *vor-**raym**-mo la kolats-**yoh**nay/oona bot-**teel**-ya dee veeno nayl-la nostra **ka**mayra*
Put it on my bill	**Lo metta sul mio conto** *lo mayt-ta sool mee-o kohntoh*
I'd like an outside line, please	**Mi dà la linea, per favore** *mee dah la **lee**nay-a payr la-**voh**ray*
I have lost my key	**Ho perso la mia chiave** *o payrso la mee-a kee-**ah**vay*
I have locked myself out of my room	**Sono rimasto chiuso fuori della mia stanza** *sohnoh ree-**mas**to kee-**oo**zo twooree dayl-la mee-a stantsa*
What's the voltage?	**Che voltaggio è?** *kay vol**tad**-jo e*
May I have an extra blanket/an extra pillow?	**Posso avere un'altra coperta/un altro guanciale?** *pos-so a-**vay**ray oonal-tra ko-**payr**ta/oon altro gwan-**chah**lay*
The TV/radio does not work	**La TV/radio non funziona** *la tee**voo**/rahd-yo nohn foonts-**yoh**na*
Can you send someone to collect my luggage?	**Potrebbe mandare qualcuno a prendere i miei bagagli?** *po**treb**-bay man-**dah**ray kwal-**koo**no a **pren**-dayray ee mee-**ay**-ee ba**gal**-yee*

See also **COMPLAINTS, HOTEL DESK, TELEPHONE**

SELF-CATERING

Streetwise

Italian houses are not normally equipped with kettles so be prepared to boil water in a saucepan.

We've booked an apartment in the name of ...

Abbiamo prenotato un appartamento a nome di ...
ab-yahmo prayno-tahto oon ap-parta-maynto a nohmay dee ...

Which is the key for the front door?

Qual'è la chiave della porta principale?
kwahle la kee-ahvay dayl-la porta preenchee-pahlay

Where is the electricity meter?

Dov'è il contatore dell'elettricità?
dohve eel konta-tohray dayl-laylet-treechee-ta

How does the shower work?

Come funziona la doccia?
kohmay foonts-yohna la dot-cha

Is there a cleaner?

C'è un'addetta alle pulizie?
che oonad-dayt-ta allay pooleet-see-ay

Is the cost of electricity included in the rental?

Nell'affitto è compresa la luce?
nel-laf-feet-to e kom-prayza la loochay

Is there any spare bedding?

Ci sono altre lenzuola e coperte?
chee sohnoh altray laynt-swola ay ko-payrtay

The toilet does not work

Il gabinetto non funziona
eel gabee-nayt-to nohn foonts-yohna

A fuse has blown

È fuso un fusibile
e foozo oon foozee-beelay

Where can I contact you?

Dove posso mettermi in contatto con lei?
dohvay pos-so mayt-tayrmee een kontat-to kohn le-ee

Streetwise

Shops are generally open 0830-1300 and 1600-1930 Mon.-Sat. (though closed one day during the week) but hours vary from region to region. Department stores can provide excellent value for money - try branches of Upim and Standa. Bargains are also to be found at local markets - most towns have at least one every week.

Where is the main shopping area?	**Dove sono i negozi principali?** *dohvay sohnoh ee nay-**got**see preenchee-**pah**lee*
Where are the big stores?	**Dove sono i grandi magazzini?** *dohvay sohnoh ee grandee magadz-**zee**nee*
What time do the shops close?	**A che ora chiudono i negozi?** *a kay ohra kee-**oo**-dohnoh ee nay-**got**see*
How much does that cost?	**Quanto costa quello?** *kwanto kohsta kwayl-lo*
How much is it per kilo/per metre?	**Quanto costa al chilo/al metro?** *kwanto kohsta al keelo/al metro*
Can I try it on?	**Posso provarlo?** *pos-so pro-**vahr**lo*
Where is the food department?	**Dov'è il reparto alimentari?** *dohve eel ray-**par**to alee-mayn-**tah**ree*
I'm looking for a gift for my wife	**Sto cercando un regalo per mia moglie** *sto chayr-**kan**do oon ray-**gah**lo payr mee-a mol-yay*
I'm just looking	**Sto guardando solamente** *sto gwar-**dan**do sola-**mayn**tay*
Could I have a carrier bag?	**Potrei avere una busta di plastica?** *po**tree**-ee a-**vay**ray oona boosta dee **pla**steeka*

SIGHTSEEING

Streetwise

Museum opening hours may be erratic and liable to change at short notice, so do check them in advance of a visit. Churches open in the early morning, but usually close for three or four hours at noon. In some cities there is one day of the month when entry to all museums is free - enquire at the local tourist office.

What is there to see here?

Che cosa c'è da vedere qui?
*kay koza che da vay-**day**ray kwee*

Excuse me, how do I get to the cathedral?

Scusi, come faccio per andare al duomo?
*skoozee kohmay fat-cho payr an-**dah**ray al dwomo*

Where is the museum/ the main square?

Dov'è il museo/la piazza principale?
*doh**ve** eel moo**ze**-o/la pee-**ats**-sa preenchee-**pah**lay*

What time does the museum open?

A che ora apre il museo?
*a kay ohra apray eel moo**ze**-o*

Is the castle open to the public?

Il castello è aperto al pubblico?
*eel ka**stel**-lo e a-**payr**to al **poob**-bleeko*

Can we take photographs in here?

Possiamo fare delle fotografie qui dentro?
*pos-**yah**mo fahray day-lay foto-gra**fee**-ay kwee dayntro*

How much does it cost to get in?

Quanto costa il biglietto di entrata?
*kwanto kohsta eel beel-**yayt**-to dee ayn-**trah**ta*

Where can I buy some film/ postcards?

Dove posso comprare un rullino/delle cartoline?
*dohvay pos-so kom-**prah**ray oon rool-**lee**no/ dayl-lay karto-**lee**nay*

See also **MAPS & GUIDES, TRIPS & EXCURSIONS**

Streetwise

Tobacconist's (tabaccherie) have a sign which is usually a black T on a white background. Most familiar brands are sold in Italy. Look out for the 'No Smoking' sign VIETATO FUMARE.

Do you mind if I smoke?	**Le dispiace se fumo?** *lay deespee-achay say foomo*
May I have an ashtray?	**Posso avere un portacenere?** *pos-so a-vayray oon porta-chay-nayray*
Is this a non-smoking compartment/area?	**Questo/Questa è uno scompartimento/una zona per non fumatori?** *kwaysto/kwaysta e oono skompar-tee-maynto/oona zona payr nohn fooma-tohree*
A packet of ..., please	**Un pachetto di ..., per favore** *oon pak-kayt-to dee ... payr fa-vohray*
Have you got any American/English cigarettes?	**Avete delle sigarette americane/inglesi?** *a-vaytay dayl-lay seega-ret-tay amay-roe kahnay/een-glayzee*
I'd like some pipe tobacco	**Vorrei del tabacco per la pipa** *vor-re-ee dayl tabak-ko payr la peepa*
Do you have any matches/pipe cleaners?	**Avete dei fiammiteri/dogli scovolini?** *a-vaytay day-ee fee-am-mee-fayray/dayl-lyee skovo-leence*
Have you a gas refill for my lighter?	**Avete una bomboletta di gas per il mio accendino?** *a-vaytay oona bombo-layt-ta dee gas payr eel mee-o at-chayn-deeno*
Have you got a light?	**Ha da accendere?** *a da at-chen-dayray*

SPORTS

| Which sports activities are available here? | **Quali sport si possono fare qui?** |
| | *kwahlee sport see **pos**-sono fahray kwee* |

| Is it possible to go fishing/riding? | **Si può andare a pescare/a cavallo?** |
| | *see pwo an-**dah**ray a pay-**skah**ray/a kaval-lo* |

| Where can we play tennis/golf? | **Dove possiamo giocare a tennis/a golf?** |
| | *dohvay pos-**yah**mo jo-**kah**ray a ten-nees/a golf* |

| Are there any interesting walks nearby? | **Ci sono delle belle passeggiate da fare qui vicino?** |
| | *chee sohnoh dayl-lay bel-lay pas-sayd-**jah**tay da fahray kwee vee-**chee**no* |

| Can we hire the equipment? | **Possiamo noleggiare le attrezzature?** |
| | *pos-**yah**mo nolayd-**jah**ray at-trayts-sa-**too**ray* |

| How much does it cost per hour? | **Quanto costa all'ora?** |
| | *kwanto kohsta al-**loh**ra* |

| Do we need to be members? | **Bisogna essere soci?** |
| | *bee**zohn**-ya es-**say**ray sochee* |

| Where do we buy our tickets? | **Dove si comprano i biglietti?** |
| | *dohvay see **kohm**-prano ee beel-**yayt**-tee* |

| Can we take lessons? | **Possiamo prendere delle lezioni?** |
| | *pos-**yah**mo **pren**-dayray dayl-lay layts-**yoh**nee* |

See also **BEACH, ENTERTAINMENT, WATERSPORTS, WINTER SPORTS**

Streetwise

*As a rule, taxis should be picked up at a stand rather than hailed.
Make sure you are taking an official taxi (usually yellow) - pirate cab
operators are likely to overcharge you. Tips should be around 15% of
the total fare.*

Can you order me a taxi, please?	**Può chiamarmi un taxi, per favore?** *pwo kee-a-**mahr**mee oon taxee payr fa-**voh**ray*
To the main station	**Alla stazione centrale** *al-la stats-**yoh**nay chayn-**trah**lay*
Take me to this address	**Mi porti a quest'indirizzo** *mee portee a kwaysteen-dee**reets**-so*
Is it far?	**È lontano?** *e lon-**tah**no*
How much will it cost?	**Quanto verrà a costare?** *kwanto ver-**ra** a ko-**stah**ray*
I'm in a hurry	**Ho molta fretta** *o **moh**lta fray-ta*
Can you wait here for a few minutes?	**Può aspettare qui per alcuni minuti?** *pwo aspayt-**tah**ray kwee payr al-**koo**nee mee-**noo**tee*
Turn left/right here	**Adesso giri a sinistra/a destra** *ades-so jeeree a see-**nee**stra/a destra*
Please stop here/ at the corner	**Si fermi qui/all'angolo per favore** *see fayrmee kwee/al-**lan**-golo payr fa-**voh**ray*
Can you give me a receipt?	**Può farmi una ricevuta?** *pwo fahrmee oona reechay-**voo**ta*

TELEPHONE

Streetwise

Most public telephones take 100- , 200- and 500-lire coins. Older telephones take gettoni (tokens) which you can buy from post offices, tobacconist's, bars and some newspaper kiosks for 200 lire each. Phonecards are now widely available. Long-distance calls are best made from telephones in main post offices and SIP offices which work a scatti - you make your call in a booth and are then charged for the number of units (scatti) you have used. To call abroad, dial 00 before the country code. To call the UK, dial 00 44 then the area code without the first 0. Thus to call London, dial 00 44 171 or 181 and then the number you require.

I want to make a phone call	**Voglio fare una telefonata** *vol-yo fahray oona taylay-fo-**nah**ta*
Can I have a line?	**Posso avere la linea?** *pos-so a-**vay**ray la **lee**nay-a*
The number is ..., extension ...	**Il numero è ..., interno ...** (*see* NUMBERS) *eel **noo**-mayro e ... een-**tayr**no ...*
I want to reverse the charges	**Voglio addebitare la spesa al ricevente** *vol-yo ad-daybee-**tah**ray la spayza al reechay-**ven**tay*
Have you got a telephone?	**C'è un telefono?** *che oon tay**le**-fono*
How much is it to phone England?	**Quanto costa telefonare in Inghilterra?** *kwanto kohsta taylay-fo-**nah**ray een eengeel-**ter**-ra*
I can't get through	**Non riesco a prendere la linea** *nohn ree-esko a **pren**-dayray la **lee**nay-a*
The line's engaged	**La linea è occupata** *la **lee**nay-a e ok-koo-**pah**ta*

Hello, this is ...

Pronto, sono ...
prohntoh sohnoh ...

Can I speak to ...?

Posso parlare con ...?
pos-so par-lahray kohn ...

I've been cut off

Mi è stata tolta la communicazione
mee e stahta tolta la kom-moonee-kats-yohnay

It's a bad line

Si sente male
see sayntay mahlay

YOU MAY HEAR:

Sto cercando di mettervi in communicazione
sto chayr-kando dee mayt-tayrvee een komoo-neekats-yohnay

I'm trying to connect you

La sto mettendo in linea
la sto mayt-tayndo een leenay-a

I'm putting you through

Resti in linea
raystee een leenay-a

Hold the line

Mi dispiace, è occupato
mee deespee-achay e ok-koo-pahto

I'm sorry, it's engaged

Riprovi più tardi per favore
ree-prohvee pee-oo tardee payr fa-vohray

Please try again later

Chi chiama?
kee kee-ahma

Who's calling?

Scusi, ho sbagliato numero
skoozee, o zbal-yahto noo-mayro

Sorry, wrong number

TIME

Streetwise

The 24-hour clock is used widely; thus, you may hear:

le ore ventuno	2100	9.00 pm
*lay ohray ven-**too**no*		
le diciasette meno un quarto	1645	4.45 pm
*lay deecha-**set**-tay mayno oon kwarto*		

What's the time?
Che ora è?/Che ore sono?
kay ohra eh/kay ohray sohnoh

It's ...
È/Sono ...
eh/sohnoh

8.00	**le otto**
	lay ot-to
8.05	**le otto e cinque**
	lay ot-to ay cheen-kway
8.10	**le otto e dieci**
	*lay ot-to ay dee-**e**-chee*
8.15	**le otto e un quarto**
	lay ot-to ay oon kwarto
8.20	**le otto e venti**
	lay ot-to ay vayntee
8.25	**le otto e venticinque**
	*lay ot-to ay vayntee-**cheen**-kway*
8.30	**le otto e mezza**
	lay ot-to ay medz-za
8.35	**le nove meno venticinque**
	*lay novay mayno vayntee-**cheen**-kway*
8.40	**le nove meno venti**
	lay novay mayno vayntee
8.45	**le nove meno un quarto**
	lay novay mayno oon kwarto
8.50	**le nove meno dieci**
	*lay novay mayno dee-**e**-chee*
8.55	**le nove meno cinque**
	lay novay mayno cheen-kway
midday	**mezzogiorno**
	*medz-zo-**jor**no*
midnight	**mezzanotte**
	*medz-za-**not**-tay*

See also **NUMBERS**

What time do you
open/close?

A che ora apre/chiude?
a kay ohra apray/kee-ooday

Do we have time to
visit the town?

Abbiamo tempo per visitare la città?
ab-yahmo tempo payr veezee-tahray la cheet-ta

How long will it
take to get there?

Quanto ci vorrà per arrivarci?
kwanto chee vor-ra payr ar-ree-vahrchee

We can be there in
half an hour

Possiamo arrivarci in mezz'ora
pos-yahmo ar-ree-vahrchee een medz-zohra

We arrived early/
late

Siamo arrivati presto/tardi
see-ahmo ar-ree-vahtee presto/tardee

We must be back at
the hotel before
... o'clock

**Dobbiamo essere in albergo prima
delle ...** (see TIME)
*dob-yahmo es-sayray een al-bayrgo preema
dayl-lay ...*

When does the
coach leave in the
morning?

A che ora parte l'autobus alla mattina?
a kay ohra partay lowto-boos al-la mat-teena

The table is booked
for ... o'clock this
evening

**Il tavolo è riservato per le ... di questa
sera** (see TIME)
*eel tah-volo e reezayr-vahto payr lay ...
dee kwaysta sayra*

We'll be back very
late

Torneremo molto tardi
tornay-raymo mohltoh tahrdee

We'll be staying
for a week/
until ...

Resteremo per una settimana/fino al ...
(see DATE & CALENDAR)
*raystay-raymo payr oona sayt-tee-mahna/
feeno al ...*

TIPPING

Streetwise

*Your bill in cafes and restaurants will include a service charge -
Servizio Compreso (Service Included) - but any special service should
be tipped for separately. In addition, it is usual to leave the waiter any
small coins from your change. Porters and chambermaids in hotels
should also be tipped, as should lavatory attendants.*

Sorry, I don't have any change	**Mi dispiace, non ho spiccioli** *mee deespee-achay nohn o **speet**-cholee*
Could you give me change of ...?	**Mi può dare ... in moneta?** (see NUMBERS) *mee pwo dahray ... een mo-nayta*
Is it usual to tip ...?	**Si deve dare la mancia di ...?** *see dayvay dahray la mancha dee ...*
How much should I tip?	**Quanto devo lasciare di mancia?** *kwanto dayvo la-**shah**ray dee mancha*
Keep the change	**Tenga pure il resto** *tenga pooray eel resto*
Make it ... lire	**Faccia ... lire** (see NUMBERS) *fat-cha ... leeray*

See also **TAXIS, TOILETS**

Streetwise

Toilets which are attended are generally much cleaner and will have toilet paper, soap and towels, Items which are frequently missing from other public conveniences. You should tip the attendant on leaving (minimum of L.200).

Where are the toilets, please?	**Dov'è la toilette, per favore** *dohve la twalet payr fa-vohray*
Where is the Gents'/ the Ladies'?	**Dov'è la toilette per Signori/per Signore?** *dohve la twalet payr seen-yohree/seen-yohray*
Do you have to pay?	**Bisogna pagare?** *beezohn-ya pa-gahray*
This toilet does not flush	**L'acqua non esce da questo water** *lakwa nohn e-shay da kwaysto vatayr*
There is no toilet paper/soap	**Non c'è carta igienica/sapone** *nohn che kahrta ee-je-neeka/sa-pohnay*
Do I have to pay extra to use the washbasin?	**Bisogna pagare di più per usare il lavandino?** *beezohn-ya pa-gahray dee pee-oo payr oo-zahray eel lavan-deeno*
Is there a toilet for the disabled?	**C'è una toilette per handicappati?** *che oona twalet payr andee-kap-pahtee*
Are there facilities for mothers with babies?	**Ci sono dei servizi per madri con bambini?** *chee sohnoh day-ee sayr-veetsee payr mahdree kohn bam-beenee*
The door will not close	**La porta non si chiude** *la porta nohn see kee-ooday*

TRAIN TRAVEL

Streetwise

Trains are graded as follows:
Super Rapido/Inter City - *High-speed train. Advance booking is obligatory and a supplement must be paid. First class only.*
Rapido - *High-speed train. A supplement must be paid and booking is sometimes obligatory. Mainly first class.*
Espresso - *Express; stops at main stations only. First and second class.*
Diretto - *Stops at the majority of stations. Both classes.*
Locale/Accelerato - *Stops at all stations. Both classes.*

Is this the train for ...?	**È questo il treno per ...?** *e kwaysto eel treno payr ...*
Is this seat free?	**È libero questo posto?** *e **lee**-bayro kwaysto pohstoh*
I have a seat reservation	**Ho un posto prenotato** *o oon pohstoh prayno-**tah**to*
May I open the window?	**Posso aprire il finestrino?** *pos-so a-**pree**ray eel feenay-**stree**no*
What time do we get to ...?	**A che ora arriviamo a ...?** *a kay ohra ar-reev-**yah**mo a ...*
Do we stop at ...?	**Ci fermiamo a ...?** *chee fayrm-**yah**mo a ...*
Where do I change for ...?	**Dove devo cambiare per ...?** *dohvay dayvo kamb-**yah**ray payr ...*
Is there a buffet car/ restaurant car?	**C'è una carrozza con ristorante?** *che oona kar-**rots**-sa kohn reesto-**ran**tay*
Please tell me when we get to ...	**Per favore mi dica quando arriviamo a ...** *payr fa-**voh**ray mee deeka kwando ar-reev-**yah**mo a ...*

See also **LUGGAGE, RAILWAY STATION**

TRAVEL AGENT

What's the best way to get to ...?	**Qual'è il modo migliore per andare a ...?** *kwahle eel modoh meel-yohray payr an-dahray a ...*
How much is it to fly to ...?	**Quanto costa andare in aereo a ...?** *kwanto kohsta an-dahray een a-e-ray-o a ...*
Are there any special cheap fares?	**Ci sono delle tariffe speciali?** *chee sohnoh dayl-lay tareef-fay spay-chahlee*
What times are the trains/flights?	**A che ora ci sono i treni/i voli?** *a kay ohra chee sohnoh ee trenee/ee vohlee*
Can I buy the tickets here?	**Posso comprare qui i biglietti?** *pos-so kom-prahray kwee ee beel-yayt-tee*
Can I change my booking?	**Posso cambiare la mia prenotazione?** *pos-so kamb-yahray la mee-a prayno-tats-yohnay*
Can you book me on the London flight?	**Può prenotarmi un posto sul volo di Londra?** *pwo prayno-tahrmee oon pohstoh sool vohlo dee lohndra*
Can I get back to Manchester tonight?	**Posso ritornare a Manchester questa notte?** *pos-so reetor-nahray a manchester kwaysta not-tay*
Two second class returns to ..., please	**Due biglietti di andata e ritorno, seconda classe per ..., per favore** *doo-ay beel-yayt-tee dee an-dahtee ay ree-torno say-kohnda klas-say payr ... payr fa-vohray*
Can you book me into a hotel?	**Può prenotarmi un posto in albergo?** *pwo prayno-tahrmee oon pohstoh een al-bayrgo*

TRIPS & EXCURSIONS

Are there any
sightseeing tours?

Ci sono delle gite turistiche?
chee sohnoh dayl-lay jeetay tooree-steekay

When is the bus
tour of the town?

**Quando inizia il giro della città in
autobus?**
*kwando eeneets-ya eel jeero dayl-la cheet-ta
een ow-toboos*

How long does the
tour take?

Quanto dura la gita?
kwanto doora la jeeta

Are there any boat
trips on the river/
lake?

**Ci sono delle gite in barca sul fiume/sul
lago?**
*chee sohnoh dayl-lay jeetay een barka sool
fee-oomay/sool lahgo*

Are there any
guided tours of
the cathedral?

Ci sono delle visite guidate del duomo?
*chee sohnoh dayl-lay vee-zeetay gwee-dahtay
dayl dwomo*

Is there a reduction
for senior citizens/
children/groups?

**C'è una riduzione per pensionati/
bambini/i gruppi?**
*che oona reedoots-yohnay payr
payns-yo-nahtee/bam-beenee/ee groop-pee*

Is there a commentary
in English?

C'è un commento in inglese?
che oon kom-maynto een een-glayzay

Where do we stop
for lunch?

Dove ci fermiamo per la colazione?
*dohvay chee fayrm-yahmo payr la
kolats-yohnay*

See also **SIGHTSEEING**

Is it possible to go water-skiing/ windsurfing?	**Si può fare lo sci d'acqua/windsurf?** *see pwo fahray loh shee dakwa/windsurf*
Can we rent a motor boat/rowing boat?	**Possiamo affittare una barca a motore/ una barca a remi?** *pos-yahmo af-feet-tahray oona barka a moh-tohray/oona barka a raymee*
Can I rent a sailboard?	**Posso affittare una tavola per il surf?** *pos-so af-feet-tahray oona tah-vola payr eel surf*
Can one swim in the river?	**Si può nuotare nel fiume?** *see pwo nwo-tahray nayl fee-oomay*
Can we fish here?	**Possiamo pescare qui?** *pos-yahmo pay-skahray kwee*
Is there a paddling pool for the children?	**C'è una piscina per bambini?** *che oona pee-sheena payr bam-beenee*
Do you give lessons?	**Dà lezioni?** *da layts-yohnee*
Where is the municipal swimming pool?	**Dov'è la piscina pubblica?** *dohve la pee-sheena poob-bleeka*
Is the pool heated?	**È riscaldata la piscina?** *e reeskal-dahta la pee-sheena*
Is it an outdoor pool?	**È una piscina all'aperto?** *e oona pee-sheena al-lapayr-to*

See also **BEACH**

WEATHER

It's a lovely day

È una bella giornata
e oona bel-la jor-nahta

It's sunny

C'è il sole
che eel sohlay

What dreadful
weather!

Che tempo brutto!
kay tempo broot-to

It is raining/
snowing

Piove/nevica
pee-ovay/nay-veeka

It's windy

C'è vento
che vento

There's a nice
breeze blowing

C'è un bel venticello
che oon bel vayntee-chayl-lo

Will it be cold
tonight?

Farà freddo stasera?
fara fred-do sta-sayra

Is it going to rain/
to snow?

Pioverà/nevicherà?
pee-ovay-ra/nayvee-kayra

Will there be a
thunderstorm?

Ci sarà un temporale?
chee sara oon taympo-rahlay

Is it going to be
fine?

Sarà una bella giornata?
sara oona bel-la jor-nahta

Is the weather
going to change?

Il tempo cambierà?
eel tempo kamb-yayra

What is the
temperature?

Quanti gradi ci sono?
kwantee gradee chee sohnoh

Italy produces more wine than any other country and names like *Chianti, Lambrusco* and *Frascati* are known throughout the world. In Italy wine is normally drunk with meals but is also taken as an aperatif (particularly in the north) and with desserts. All bars and cafes are licensed to sell alcohol and one can have a glass of wine or spirits at any time of the day. *Osterie* (type of pub) and *enoteche* (wine bars) have wine on tap and sell a huge range of Italian and foreign wines.

Each region has its own particular wines. Among the most famous are:

> *Marsala* - a dessert wine from Sicily
> *Frascati* - a white wine from near Rome
> *Verdicchio* - a dry white wine from the Marche
> *Chianti* and *Brunello di Montalcino* - red wines from Tuscany
> *Lambrusco* - a sparkling red wine from Emilia-Romagna
> *Barolo, Barbera* and *Nebbiolo* (dry red wines) and *Asti Spumante* (a sparkling white wine); all from Piedmont
> *Bardolino, Valpolicella* (red) and *Soave* (white) - all from the Verona area

You'll often see the letters *DOC* on the label of a wine bottle: this stands for *denominazione di origine controllata* and means that the wine has been produced with high quality grapes and that a quality control has been carried out to verify this. Even higher standards of quality control have been applied to wines which bear the symbol *DOCG (denominazione di origine controllata e garantita)*.

When eating out you may see on the menu *il vino della casa* (the house wine). House wines are well worth trying as they are normally cheaper than bottled wines without being of inferior quality. Ask for *una caraffa del vino della casa* (a carafe of the house wine), or for *una caraffa da mezzo litro* (a half-litre carafe) or *una caraffa da un quarto* (a quarter-litre carafe).

Most well-known brands of spirits are available in Italy. If you want to try something particularly Italian, ask for a glass of *grappa*, a strong (very strong!) white spirit made from grape pressings.

We'd like an aperitif	**Vorremmo un aperitivo** *vor-**raym**-mo oon a-payree-**tee**vo*
May I have the wine list?	**Posso avere la lista dei vini?** *pos-so a-**vay**ray la leesta dayee veenee*
Can you recommend a good red/white/ rosé wine?	**Ci può consigliare un buon vino rosso/ bianco/rosato?** *che pwo konseel-**yah**ray oon bwon veeno ros-so/bee-**an**ko/ro-**zah**to*
A bottle/carafe of house wine	**Una bottiglia/una caraffa di vino della casa** *oona bot-**teel**-ya/oona ka**raf**-fa dee veeno dayl-la kasa*
A half bottle of ...	**Mezza bottiglia di ...** *medz-za bot-**teel**-ya dee ...*
Would you bring another glass, please?	**Può portare un altro bicchiere per favore?** *pwo por-**tah**ray oon altro beek-**ye**-ray payr fa-**voh**ray*
This wine is not chilled	**Questo vino non è stato messo al fresco** *kwaysto veeno nohn e stahto mays-so al fraysko*
What liqueurs do you have?	**Quali liquori avete?** *kwahlee lee-**kwoh**ree a-**vay**tay*
I'll have a brandy/ scotch/gin and tonic	**Prendo un brandy/un whisky/un gin con acqua tonica** *prendo oon brandy/oon wheeskee/oon jeen kohn ak-kwa **to**-neeka*
A Campari and soda	**Un Campari con seltz** *oon campari kohn selts*

See also **EATING OUT, MENUS, ORDERING**

Can we hire skis here?

Possiamo noleggiare degli sci qui?
pos-yahmo nolayd-jahray dayl-yee shee kwee

Could you adjust my bindings?

Può regolare i miei attacchi?
pwo raygo-lahray ee mee-e-ee at-tak-kee

A one-week ticket, please

Un biglietto valido per una settimana, per favore
oon beel-yayt-to va-leedo payr oona sayt-tee-mahna payr fa-vohray

What are the snow conditions?

Com'è la neve?
kolime la nayvay

The snow is very icy/heavy

La neve è molto ghiacciata/pesante
la nayvay e mohltoh gee-at-chahta/pay-zantay

Is there a restaurant at the top station?

C'è un ristorante alla stazione d'arrivo?
che oon reesto-rantay al-la stats-yohnay dar-reevo

Which are the easiest runs?

Quali sono le piste più facili?
kwahlee sohnoh lay peestay pee-oo fa-cheelee

We'll take the gondola

Prendiamo la seggiovia
prend-yahmo la sayd-jovee-a

When is the last ascent?

Quand'è l'ultima salita?
kwan-de lool-teema sa-leeta

Is there danger of avalanches?

C'è pericolo di valanghe?
che payree-kolo dee va-langay

a un, una *oon, oona*

abbey l'abbazia *(f) ab-batsee-a*

about: a book about Venice un libro su Venezia *oon leebro soo vaynayts-ya*; **about ten o'clock** circa le dieci *cheerka lay dee-echee*

above sopra *sohpra*

accident l'incidente *(m) eenchee-dentay*

accommodation l'alloggio *(m) al-lod-jo*

ache fare male *fahray mahlay*; **my head aches** mi fa male la testa *mee fa mahlay la testa*

adaptor *(electrical)* il riduttore *reedoot-tohray*

address l'indirizzo *(m) eendee-reets-so*

adhesive tape il nastro adesivo *nastro aday-zeevo*

admission charge il prezzo del biglietto d'ingresso *prets-so dayl beel-yayt-to deengres-so*

adult l'adulto *(m) a-doolto*

advance: in advance in anticipo *een antee-cheepo*

after dopo *dohpoh*

afternoon il pomeriggio *pomay-reed-jo*

aftershave il dopobarba *dopo-bahrba*

again ancora *an-kora*

agent l'agente *(m/f) a-jentay*

ago: a week ago una settimana fa *oona sayt-tee-mahna fa*

air-conditioning l'aria *(f)* condizionata *ahree-a kohndeets-*

air-line *(tube)* il tubo dell'aria *toobo dayl-lahree-a*

air mail via aerea *vee-a-ayray-a*

air-mattress il materassino gonfiabile *matay-ras-seeno gonfee-ah-beelay*

airport l'aeroporto *(m) a-ay-ropor-to*

aisle il passaggio *pas-sad-jo*

alarm l'allarme *(m) al-lahrmay*

alcohol l'alcool *(m) alko-ol*

alcoholic alcolico *alko-leeko*

all tutto *toot-to*

allergic allergico *al-layr-jeeko*

allowance *(customs)* la quantità permessa *kwantee-ta payrmays-sa*

all right *(agreed)* va bene *va benay*; **are you all right?** stai bene? *sta-ee benay*

almost quasi *kwahzee*

also anche *ankay*

always sempre *saympray*

am *see GRAMMAR*

ambulance l'ambulanza *(f) amboo-lantsa*

America l'America *(f) amay-reeka*

American americano *amay-ree-kahno*

anaesthetic l'anestetico *(m) anay-ste-teeko*

and e *ay*

anorak la giacca a vento *jak-ka a vento*

another un altro *oon altro*; **another beer?** ancora una birra? *an-kohra oona beer-ra*

antibiotic l'antibiotico *(m) antee-bee-o-teeko*

antifreeze l'antigelo *(m) antee-jaylo*

antiseptic l'antisettico *(m) antee-set-teeko*

any dei/delle; **I haven't any money** non ho soldi *nohn o soldee*

apartment l'appartamento *(m) ap-parta-maynto*

aperitif l'aperitivo *(m) a-payree-teevo*

apple la mela *mayla*

appointment l'appuntamento *(m) ap-puonta-maynto*

apricot l'albicorca *(f) albee-kok-ka*

are see GRAMMAR

arm il braccio *brat-cho*

armbands *(for swimming)* i braccial *brat-chahlee*

arrivals gli arrivi *ar-reevee*

arrive arrivare *ar-ree-vahray*

art gallery la galleria d'arte *gallayree-a dartay*

artichoke il carciofo *kar-chohfo*

ashtray il portacenere *porta-chay-nayray*

asparagus gli asparagi *aspa-rajee*

aspirin l'aspirina *(f) aspee-reena*

asthma l'asma *(f) azma*

at a *a*; **at home** a casa *a kahsa*

aubergine la melanzana *maylant-sahna*

Australia l'Australia *(f) owstrahl-ya*

Australian australiano/a *ow-stral-yahno/a*

automatic automatico *owto-ma-teeko*

autumn autunno *owtoon-no*

avalanche la valanga *va-langa*

avocado l'avocado *avo-kahdo*

baby il bambino *bam-beeno*

baby food gli alimenti per bambini *alee-mayntee payr bam-beenee*

babysitter il/la baby-sitter *baby-sittor*

back n *(of body)* la schiena *skee-e-na*

backpack lo zaino *dza-eeno*

bacon la pancetta *panchayt-ta*

bad *(food)* guasto *gwasto*; *(weather, news)* brutto *broot-to*

bag la borsa *borsa*; *(suitcase)* la valigia *va-leeja*

baggage i bagagli *bagal-yee*

baggage reclaim il ritiro bagagli *ree-teero bagal-yee*

baker's la panetteria *panayt-tay-ree-a*

balcony il balcone *bal-kohnay*

ball la palla *pal-la*

banana la banana *ba-nana*

band *(musical)* la banda *banda*

bandage la benda *benda*

bank la banca *hanka*

bar il bar *bar*

barber il barbiere *barb-yeray*

basket il cestino *chay-steeno*

bath il bagno *ban-yo*; **to take a bath** fare un bagno *fahray oon ban-yo*

bathing cap la cuffia *koof-ya*

bathroom il bagno *ban-yo*

battery la batteria *bat-tayree-a*

be see GRAMMAR

beach la spiaggia *spee-ad-ja*

beans i fagioli *fa-jolee*

beautiful bello *bel-lo*

bed il letto *let-to*

bedding la biancheria *bee-ankay-ree-a*

bedroom la camera da letto *ka-mayra da let-to*

beef il manzo *mandzo*

beer la birra *beer-ra*

beetroot la barbabietola *bahrbab-ye-tola*

before prima di *preema dee*

begin cominciare *komeen-chahray*

behind dietro di *dee-etro dee*

below sotto *soht-to*

belt la cintura *cheen-toora*

beside accanto a *ak-kanto a*

best migliore *meel-yohray*

better (than) meglio (di) *mel-yo (dee)*

between fra *fra*

bicycle la bicicletta *beechee-klayt-ta*

big grande *granday*

bigger più grande *pee-oo granday*

bikini il bikini *bee-keenee*

bill il conto *kohntoh*

bin il bidone *bee-dohnay*

binoculars il binocolo *beeno-kolo*

bird l'uccello (*m*) *oot-chel-lo*

birthday il compleanno *komplay-an-no*

birthday card il biglietto di auguri di buon compleanno *beel-yayt-to dee owgoo-ree dee bwon komplay-an-no*

bit il pezzo *pets-so*; **a bit of** un po' di *oon po dee*

bitten morso *morso*; (by insect) punto *poonto*

bitter amaro *a-mahro*

black nero *nayro*

blackcurrant il ribes nero *reebes nayro*

blanket la coperta *ko-payrta*

bleach la candeggina *kanday-jeena*

blocked bloccato *blok-kahto*

blood group il gruppo sanguigno *groop-po sangween-yo*

blouse la camicetta *kamee-chayt-ta*

blow-dry asciugare con il föhn *ashoo-gahray kohn eel fon*

blue blu *bloo*

boarding card la carta d'imbarco *karta deem-barko*

boarding house la pensione *paynsee-ohnay*

boat la barca *barka*

boat trip la gita in barca *jeeta een barka*

boiled bollito *bol-leeto*

book[1] *n* il libro *leebro*

book[2] *vb* prenotare *prayno-tahray*

booking la prenotazione *prayno-tats-yohnay*

booking office la biglietteria *beel-yayt-tayree-a*

book of tickets il blocchetto di biglietti *blok-kayt-to dee beel-yayt-tee*

bookshop libreria *leebray-ree-a*

boots gli stivali *stee-vahlee*

border la frontiera *front-yera*

both tutti e due *toot-tee ay doo-ay*

bottle la bottiglia *bot-teel-ya*

bottle opener l'apribottiglie (*m*) *apree-bot-teel-yay*

box la scatola *skah-tola*

box office il botteghino *bot-tay-geeno*

boy il ragazzo *ragats-so*
boyfriend il ragazzo *ragats-so*
bra il reggiseno *rayd-jee-sayno*
bracelet il braccialetto *brat-chalayt-to*
brake fluid l'olio *(m)* per i freni *ol-yo payr ee fraynee*
brakes i freni *fraynee*
brandy brandy *brandy*
bread il pane *pahnay*
breakable fragile *fra-jeelay*
breakdown il guasto *gwasto*
breakdown van il carro attrezzi *karro at-trayts-see*
breakfast la colazione *kola-tsyohnay*
breast *(chicken)* il petto *payt-to*
briefcase la cartella *kartel-la*
bring portare *por-tahray*
Britain La Gran Bretagna *gran braytan-ya*
British britannico *breetan-neeko*
brochure il dépliant *dayplee-on*
broken rotto *roht-to*
broken down *(machine, car)* guasto *gwasto*
brooch la spilla *speel-la*
broom la scopa *skohpa*
brother il fratello *fratel-lo*
brown marrone *mar-rohnay*
brush la spazzola *spats-sola*
Brussels sprouts i cavoletti di Bruxelles *kahvo-layt-tee dee brooksel*
bucket il secchiello *sek-yayl-lo*
buffet il buffet *boo-fe*
buffet car la carrozza ristorante

kar-rots-sa reesto-rantay
bulb la lampadina *lampa-deena*
bun il panino dolce *pa-neeno dohlchay*
bureau de change l'ufficio *(m)* di cambio *oof-feecho dee kamb-yo*
burst scoppiato *skop-yahto*
bus l'autobus *(m)* *ow tohpos*
business gli affari *af-fahree*
bus station la stazione delle autolinee *stats-yohnay dayl-lay owto-leenay-ay*
bus stop la fermata (dell'autobus) *fayr-mahta (dayl-low-toboos)*
bus tour la gita in pullman *jeeta een poolman*
busy occupato *ok-koo-pahto*
but ma *ma*
butcher il macellaio *machayl-la-yo*
butter il burro *boor-ro*
button il bottone *bot-tohnay*
buy comprare *kom prahray*
by *(close to)* vicino a *vee-cheeno a*; *(via)* via *vee-a*; *(beside)* accanto a *ak-kanto a*
bypass la strada di circonvallazione *strahda dee cheerkon-val-lats-yohnay*

cabaret il cabaret *kaba-re*
cabbage il cavolo *kah-volo*
cablecar la funivia *foonee-vee-a*
café il caffè *kaf-fe*
cagoule la giacca a vento *jak-ka a vento*
cake la torta *torta*
call[1] *vb* chiamare *keea-mahray*
call[2] *n* *(on telephone)* la chiamata

keea-mahta; **a long-distance call** una chiamata interurbana *keea-mahta eentayr-oor-bahna*

calm calmo *kalmo*

camera la macchina fotografica *mak-keena foto-gra-feeka*

camp campeggiare *kampayd-jahray*

camp site il campeggio *kampayd-jo*

can[1] *n* il barattolo *barat-tolo*

can[2] *vb* : **can I ...?** posso ...? *pos-so*

Canada il Canada *kana-da*

Canadian Canadese *kana-dayzay*

cancel cancellare *kanchayl-lahray*

canoe la canoa *kano-a*

canoeing il canoismo *ka-no-eezmo*

can opener l'apriscatole *(m)* *apree-ska-tohlay*

car la macchina *mak-keena*

carafe la caraffa *karaf-fa*

caravan la roulotte *roolot*

carburettor il carburatore *kahrboo-ra-tohray*

card *(greetings)* la cartolina *karto-leena*; *(playing)* la carta da gioco *karta da joko*

cardigan il cardigan *cardigan*

careful attento *at-taynto*

car ferry il traghetto *tragayt-to*

car park il parcheggio *parkayd-jo*

carpet il tappeto *tap-payto*

carriage *(railway)* la carrozza *kar-rots-sa*

carrots le carote *ka-rotay*

carry portare *por-tahray*

car wash il lavaggio auto *lavad-jo ow-to*

case *(suitcase)* la valigia *va-leeja*

cash[1] *vb* *(cheque)* incassare *eenkas-sahray*

cash[2] *n* i contanti *kon-tantee*

cash desk la cassa *kas-sa*

cashier il cassiere *kas-yeray*

casino il casinò *kazee-no*

cassette la cassetta *kas-sayt-ta*

castle il castello *kastel-lo*

Catacombs le Catacombe *kata-kombay*

catch prendere *pren-dayray*

cathedral il duomo *dwomo*

Catholic cattolico *kat-to-leeko*

cauliflower il cavolfiore *kahvolf-yohray*

cave la grotta *grot-ta*

celery il sedano *se-dano*

cemetery il cimitero *cheemee-tayro*

centimetre il centimetro *chayntee-maytro*

central centrale *chayn-trahlay*

centre il centro *chentro*

cereal *(for breakfast)* i fiocchi di cereali *fee-ok-kee dee chayray-ahlee*

certain *(sure)* certo *chayrto*

certificate il certificato *chayrtee-fee-kahto*

chain la catena *ka-tayna*

chair la sedia *sed-ya*

chairlift la seggiovia *sayd-jovee-a*

chalet lo chalet *sha-le*

champagne lo champagne *shang-pan-ye*

change[1] *n* il cambio *kambyo*; *(small coins)* gli spiccioli *speet-cholee*; *(money returned)* il resto *resto*

change[2] *vb* cambiare *kamb-yahray*

changing room lo spogliatoio *spol-yato-yo*

chapel la cappella *kap pel-la*

charge la tariffa *taree f-fa*

cheap economico *ayko-no-meeko*

cheaper più economico *pee-oo ayko no-meeko*

check controllare *kontrol-lahray*

check in *(at airport)* fare il check-in *fahray eel check-in; (at hotel)* firmare il registro *feer-mahray eel ray-jeestro*

check-in desk l'accettazione *(f)* bagagli *at-chayt-tats-yohnay bagal-yee*

cheerio ciao *chao*

cheers salute *sa-lootay*

cheese il formaggio *formad-jo*

chemist's la farmacia *farma-chee-a*

cheque l'assegno *(m) as-sayn yo*

cheque book il libretto degli assegni *leebrayt-to dayl-lyee as-sayn-yee*

cheque card la carta assegni *karta as-sayn-yee*

cherries le ciliegie *cheel-yejay*

chestnut la castagna *kastan-ya*

chewing gum la gomma da masticare *gohm-ma da mastee-kahray*

chicken il pollo *pohl-lo*

chickenpox la varicella *varee-chel-la*

child *(boy)* il bambino *bam-beeno; (girl)* la bambina *bam-beena*

children *(infants)* i bambini *bam-beenee; (older children)* i ragazzi *ragats-see*

chili il peperoncino *paypay-ron-cheeno*

chips le patatine fritte *pata-teenay freet-tay*

chocolate la cioccolata *chok-ko-lahtà*

chocolates i cioccolatini *chok-kola-teenee*

Christmas Natale *(m) na-tahlay*

church la chiesa *kee-e-za*

cider il sidro *seedro*

cigar il sigaro *see-garo*

cigarette papers le cartine per sigarette *kar-teenay payr seega-rayt-tay*

cigarettes le sigarette *seega-rayt-tay*

cinema il cinema *chee-nayma*

circus il circo *cheerko*

city la città *cheet-ta*

clean[1] *adj* pulito *poo-lee-to*

clean[2] *vb* pulire *poo-leeray*

cleansing cream la crema detergente *krema daytayr-jentay*

client il/la cliente *klee-entay*

climbing l'alpinismo *(m) alpee-neezmo*

climbing boots gli scarponi da montagna *skar-pohnee da montan-ya*

cloakroom il guardaroba *gwarda-roba*

clock l'orologio *(m) oro-lojo*

close[1] *adj (near)* vicino a *vee-cheeno a*

close[2] *vb* chiudere *keeoo-dayray*

closed chiuso *kee-oozo*

cloth lo straccio *stratcho*

clothes i vestiti *vay-steetee*

clothes peg la molletta *mol-layt-ta*

cloudy nuvoloso *noovo-lohzo*

clove il chiodo *kee-odo*

club il club *kloob*

coach *(bus)* il pullman *poolman*; *(train)* la carrozza *kar-rots-sa*

coach trip la gita in pullman *jeeta een poolman*

coast la costa *kosta*

coastguard il guardacoste *gwarda-kostay*

coat il cappotto *kap-potto*

coat hanger la gruccia *grootcha*

cocktail il cocktail *cocktail*

cocoa il cacao *kaka-o*

coconut la noce di cocco *nohchay dee kok-ko*

coffee il caffè *kaf-fe*; **white coffee** il caffellatte *kaf-fay-laht-tay*; **black coffee** il caffè nero *kaf-fe nayro*

coin la moneta *mo-nayta*

Coke ® coca *ko-ka*

colander lo scolapasta *skola-pasta*

cold[1] *n* il raffreddore *raf-frayd-dohray*

cold[2] *adj* freddo *fray-do*; **I'm cold** ho freddo *o frayd-do*

Coliseum il Colosseo *kolos-sayo*

colour il colore *ko-lohray*

comb il pettine *pet-teenay*

come venire *vay-neeray*; *(arrive)* arrivare *ar-ree-vahray*; **to come back** tornare *tor-nahray*; **to come in** entrare *ayn-trahray*; **come in!** avanti! *a-vantee*

comfortable comodo *ko-modo*

company la compagnia *koınpan-yee-a*

compartment lo scompartimento *skompar-tee-maynto*

complain fare un reclamo *fahray oon ray-klahmo*

compulsory obbligatorio *ob-bleega-tor-yo*

computer il computer *komputer*

concert il concerto *kon-chayrto*

condensed milk il latte condensato *laht-tay kondaynsahto*

conditioner il balsamo *bal-samo*

conductor *(on bus)* il bigliettaio *beel-yayt-ta-yo*

conference il congresso *kongres-so*

confession la confessione *konfays-yohnay*

confirm confermare *konfayr-mahray*

congratulations le congratulazioni *kongra-toolats-yohnee*

connect collegare *kol-lay-gahray*

connection collegamento *kol-laygah-maynto*

constipated stitico *stee-teeko*

consulate il consolato *konso-lahto*

contact mettersi in contatto con *mayt-tayrsee een kontat-to kohn*

contact lens cleaner il liquido per lenti a contatto *lee-kweedo payr lentee a kontat-to*

contact lenses le lenti a contatto *lentee a kontat-to*

Continental breakfast la colazione all'europea *kolats-yohnay al-lay-ooro-pe-a*

contraceptive il contraccettivo *kontrat-chayt-teevo*

cook cucinare *koochee-nahray*

cooker la cucina *koo-cheena*

cool fresco *fraysko*

copy[1] *n* la copia *kop-ya*

copy[2] *vb* copiare *kop-yahray*

corkscrew il cavatappi *kava tap-pee*

corner l'angolo *(m) an-golo*

cornflakes i cornflakes *cornflakes*

cosmetics i cosmetici *kozmay-teechee*

cost costare *kos-tahray*; **how much does it/do they cost?** quanto costa/costano? *kwanto kosta/ko-stano*

cotton il cotone *ko-tohnay*

cotton wool il cotone idrofilo *ko tohnay eedro-feelo*

couchette la cuccetta *koot-chayt ta*

cough la tosse *tohs-say*

country *(not town)* la campagna *kampan-ya*; *(nation)* il paese *pa-ayzay*

couple *(two people)* la coppia *kop-ya*

courgettes gli zucchini *tsook-keenee*

courier il corriere *kor-yerray*

course *(of meal)* il piatto *peeat-to*

cover charge il coperto *ko-payrto*

crab il granchio *grank-yo*

crash lo scontro *skohntro*

crash helmet il casco di protezione *kasko dee protayts-yohnay*

cream *(lotion)* la crema *kre-ma*; *(on milk)* la panna *pan-na*

credit card la carta di credito *karta dee kray-deeto*

crisps le patatine *pata-teenay*

croquette la crocchetta *krok-kayt-ta*

cross *(road)* attraversare *at-travayr-*

sahray

crossed line l'interferenza *(f) eentayr-fay rentsa*

crossroads l'incrocio *(m) een-krohcho*

crowded affollato *af-fol-lahto*

cruise la crociera *kro-chera*

cucumber il cetriolo *chaytree-olo*

cup la tazza *tats-sa*

cupboard l'armadio *(m) armahd-yo*

curler il bigodino *beego-deeno*

currant la sultanina *soolta-neena*

current la corrente *kor-rayntay*

cushion il cuscino *koo-sheeno*

custard la crema pasticcera *krema pasteel-chera*

customs la dogana *do-gahna*

cut[1] *n* il taglio *tal-yo*

cut[2] *vb* tagliare *tal-yahray*

cutlery le posate *po-zahtay*

cycle la bicicletta *beechee-klayt-ta*

cycling il ciclismo *chee-kleezmo*

daily *(each day)* ogni giorno *on-yee jorno*

damage il danno *dan-no*

damp umido *oo-meedo*

dance[1] *n* il ballo *bal-lo*

dance[2] *vb* ballare *bal-lahray*

dangerous pericoloso *payree-ko-lohzo*

dark scuro *skooro*

date la data *dahta*

date of birth la data di nascita *dahta dee na-sheeta*

daughter la figlia *feel-ya*

day il giorno *jorno*

dear caro *kahro*

decaffeinated coffee il caffè decaffeinato *kaf-fe daykaf-fay-ee-nahto*

deck chair la sedia a sdraio *sed-ya a zdra-yo*

declare dichiarare *deek-ya-rahray*

deep profondo *pro-fohndo*

deep freeze il surgelatore *soorjay-la-tohray*

defrost sgelare *zjay-lahray*

de-ice liberare dal ghiaccio *leebay-rahray dayl gee-at-cho*

delay il ritardo *ree-tahrdo*

delicious delizioso *dayleets-yohzo*

dentist il/la dentista *dayn-teesta*

dentures la dentiera *daynt-yera*

deodorant il deodorante *day-oh-dohrantay*

department store il grande magazzino *granday magadz-zeeno*

departure lounge la sala d'attesa *sahla dat-tayza*

departures le partenze *partentsay*

deposit il deposito *daypo-zeeto*

dessert il dolce *dohlchay*

details i dettagli *dayt-tal-yee*

detergent il detersivo *daytayr-seevo*

detour la deviazione *dayvee-ats-yohnay*

develop sviluppare *sveeloop-pahray*

diabetic diabetico *deea-be-teeko*

dialling code il prefisso telefonico *prayfees-so taylay-fo-neeko*

diamond il diamante *dee-a-mantay*

diarrhoea la diarrea *deear-ray-a*

diary l'agenda *(f) a-jen*da

dictionary il dizionario *deets-yonahr-yo*

diesel il gasolio *gazol-yo*

diet la dieta *dee-eta*

different diverso *dee-vayrso*

difficult difficile *deef-fee-cheelay*

dinghy il canotto *kanot-to*

dining room la sala da pranzo *sahla da prantso*

dinner la cena *chayna*

direct *(train etc)* diretto *deeret-to*

directory l'elenco *(m)* telefonico *aylenko taylay-fo-neeko*

dirty sporco *sporko*

disabled handicappato *andee-kap-pahto*

disco la discoteca *deesko-teka*

discount lo sconto *skohntoh*

dish il piatto *peeat-to*

dishtowel lo strofinaccio *strofee-nat-cho*

dishwasher la lavastoviglie *lahva-stoveel-yay*

disinfectant il disinfettante *deezeen-fayt-tantay*

distilled water l'acqua *(f)* distillata *akwa deesteel-lahta*

divorced divorziato *deevorts-yahto*

dizzy stordito *stor-deeto*

do *see* GRAMMAR

doctor il medico *me-deeko*

documents i documenti *dokoo-mayntee*

doll la bambola *bam-bola*

dollars i dollari *dol-laree*

door la porta *porta*

double doppio *dop-yo*

double bed il letto matrimoniale *let-to matree-mon-yahlay*

double room la camera matrimoniale *ka mayra matree-mon-yahlay*

doughnut il krapfen *krapfen*

down giù *joo*; **to go down** (downstairs) scendere *shayn dayray*

downstairs giù *joo*

draught la corrente (d'aria) *kor-rentay (dahr-ya)*

dress[1] *n* il vestito *vay-steeto*

dress[2] *vb* : **to get dressed** vestirsi *vay-steersee*

dressing (for food) il condimento *kondee-maynto*

drink[1] *n* la bibita *bee-beeta*

drink[2] *vb* bere *bayray*

drinking chocolate la cioccolata calda *chok-ko-lahta kalda*

drinking water l'acqua (f) potabile *akwa potah-beelay*

drive guidare *gwee-dahray*

driver (of car) l'autista (m/f) *ow-teesta*

driving licence la patente *pa-tentay*

drunk ubriaco *oobree-ako*

dry[1] *adj* secco *sayk-ko*

dry[2] *vb* asciugare *ashoo-gahray*

dry cleaner's la tintoria *teento-reea*

duck l'anatra (f) *a-natra*

due: when is the train due? quando dovrebbe arrivare il treno? *kwando dovrayb-bay ar-ree-vahray eel treno*

dummy la tettarella *tayt-ta-rel-la*

during durante *doo-rantay*

duty-free esente da dogana *ay-zentay da do-gahna*

duty-free shop il duty free *duty free*

duvet il piumino *peeoo-meeno*

dynamo la dinamo *dee-namo*

each ogni *on-yee*

ear l'orecchio (m) *orayk-yo*

earache il mal d'orecchi *mal dorayk yee*

earlier più presto *pee-oo presto*

early presto *presto*

earrings gli orecchini *orayk-keenee*

east l'est (m) *est*

Easter la Pasqua *paskwa*

easy facile *fa-cheelay*

eat mangiare *man-jahray*

eel l'anguilla (f) *angweel-la*

egg l'uovo (m) *wovo*; **eggs** le uova *wova*; **fried egg** uovo fritto *wovo freet-to*; **hard-boiled egg** uovo sodo *wovo sodo*; **scrambled eggs** uova strapazzate *wova strapats-sahtay*

either: either one l'uno o l'altro *loono o laltro*

elastic l'elastico (m) *aylas-teeko*

elastic band l'elastico (m) *aylas-teeko*

electric elettrico *aylet-treeko*

electrician l'elettricista (m) *aylayt-tree-cheesta*

electricity l'elettricità (f) *aylayt-treechee-ta*

electricity meter il contatore dell'elettricità *konta-tohray dayl-laylet-treechee-ta*

electric razor il rasoio elettrico *razoyo aylet-treeko*

embassy l'ambasciata (f) *amba-shahta*

emergency l'emergenza (f) *aymayr-jentsa*

empty vuoto *vwoto*

end la fine *feenay*

engaged *(to be married)* fidanzato *feedant-sahto*; *(toilet)* occupato *ok-koo-pahto*; *(phone)* occupato *ok-koo-pahto*

engine il motore *moh-tohray*

England l'Inghilterra *(f)* *eengeel-ter-ra*

English inglese *een-glayzay*

enjoy: I enjoyed the tour la visita mi è piaciuta *la vee-zeeta mee e peea-choota*; **I enjoy swimming** mi piace nuotare *mee pee-achay nwo-tahray*

enough abbastanza *ab-bas-tantsa*

enquiry desk il banco delle informazioni *banko dayl-lay eenfor-mats-yohnay*

entertainment il divertimento *deevayr-tee-maynto*

entrance l'entrata *(f)* *ayn-trahta*

entrance fee il prezzo d'ingresso *prets-so deengres-so*

envelopes le buste *boostay*

equipment l'attrezzatura *(f)* *at-trayts-sa-toora*

escalator la scala mobile *skahla mo-beelay*

especially specialmente *spaychal-mayntay*

essential essenziale *ays-saynts-yahlay*

Eurocheque l'eurocheque *(m)* *e-ooro-chek*

Europe l'Europa *(f)* *ay-oo-ropa*

evening la sera *sayra*; **in the evening** la sera *la sayra*

evening meal la cena *chayna*

every ogni *on-yee*

everyone tutti *toot-tee*

everything tutto *toot-to*

excellent ottimo *ot-teemo*

except eccetto *ayt-chet-to*

excess luggage il bagaglio in eccedenza *bagal-yo een ayt-chay-dentsa*

exchange[1] n lo scambio *skamb-yo*

exchange[2] *vb* cambiare *kamb-yahray*

exchange rate il cambio *kamb-yo*

excursion l'escursione *(f)* *ayskoors-yohnay*

excuse scusare *skoo-zahray*; **excuse me!** *(sorry)* mi scusi! *mee skoozee*; *(when passing)* permesso! *payrmays-so*

exhaust pipe il tubo di scappamento *toobo dee skap-pa-maynto*

exhibition la mostra *mostra*

exit l'uscita *(f)* *oo-sheeta*

expensive costoso *kohs-tohzo*

expert l'esperto *(m)* *ay-spayrto*

expire *(ticket, passport)* scadere *ska-dayray*

express[1] *n* *(train)* l'espresso *(m)* *aysprays-so*

express[2] *adj* *(parcel etc)* espresso *aysprays-so*

extra *(spare)* in più *een pee-oo*; *(more)* supplementare *soop-playmayn-tahray*

eye l'occhio *(m)* *ok-yo*

eye liner la matita per occhi *ma-teeta payr ok-kee*

eye shadow l'ombretto *(m)* *ombrayt-to*

face la faccia *fat-cha*
facilities i servizi *sayr-veetsee*
faint svenire *svay-neeray*
fainted svenuto *zvay-nooto*
fair *(fun fair)* il luna-park *loona-park*
fall cadere *ka-dayray*
family la famiglia *fameel-ya*
famous famoso *fa-mohzo*
fan *(electric)* il ventilatore *vayntee-la-tohray*
fan belt la cinghia del ventilatore *cheeng-ya dayl vayntee-la-tohray*
far lontano *lon tahno*
fare la tariffa *tareef-fa*
farm la fattoria *fat-toree a*
farmhouse la cascina *ka-sheena*
fast veloce *vay-lohchay*
fat grasso *gras-so*
father il padre *pahdray*
fault *(defect)* il difetto *deefet-to*; **it's not my fault** non è colpa mia *nohn e kohlpa mee-a*
favourite preferito *prayfay-reeto*
feed dare da mangiare *dahray da man-jahray*
feel sentirsi *sayn-teersee*; **I don't feel well** non mi sento bene *nohn mee saynto benay*
ferry il traghetto *tra-gayt-to*
festival la festa *festa*
fetch *(bring)* portare *por-tahray*; *(go and get)* andare a prendere *an-dahray a pren-dayray*
fever la febbre *feb-bray*
few pochi/e *pokee/ay*; **a few** alcuni/e *al-koonee/ay*
fiancé(e) il/la fidanzato/a *feedant-sahto/a*

field il campo *kampo*
fill riempire *ree-aym-peeray*; **to fill up** *(container)* riempire *ree-aym-peeray*
fillet il filetto *feelayt-to*
film *(in cinema)* il film *feelm*; *(for camera)* la pellicola *payl-lee-kola*; *(for camera)* il rullino *rool-leeno*
filter il filtro *feeltro*
filter-tipped con filtro *kohn feeltro*
finish finire *fee-neeray*
fire il fuoco *fwoko*, **fire!** al fuoco! *al fwoko*
fire brigade i vigili del fuoco *vee-jeelee dayl fwoko*
fire extinguisher l'estintore *(m)* *aysteen-tohray*
fireworks i fuochi d'artificio *fwokee dahrtee-feecho*
first primo *preemo*
first aid il pronto soccorso *pronto sok-korso*
first class la prima classe *preema klas-say*
first floor il primo piano *preemo pee-ahno*
first name il nome di battesimo *nohmay dee bat-tay-zeemo*
fish[1] *n* il pesce *payshay*
fish[2] *vb* pescare *pay-skahray*
fit[1] *vb* *(clothes)* andare bene *an-dahray be-nay*
fit[2] *n* *(medical)* l'attacco *(m)* *at-tak-ko*
fix riparare *reepa-rahray*
fizzy frizzante *freedz-zantay*
flash il flash *flash*
flask il thermos *termos*
flat *(apartment)* l'appartamento *(m)* *ap-pahrta-maynto*

flat tyre la foratura *fo-ra-toora*
flight il volo *vohloh*
flippers le pinne *peen-nay*
floor *(of building)* il piano *pee-ahno*; *(of room)* il pavimento *pavee-maynto*
Florence Firenze *fee-rentsay*
flour la farina *fa-reena*
flowers i fiori *feeo-ree*
flu l'influenza *(f)* eenfloo-*entsa*
fly la mosca *moska*
fly sheet il soprattetto *soprat-taytto*
foggy nebbioso *nayb-yohzo*
follow seguire *say-gweeray*
food il cibo *cheebo*
food poisoning l'intossicazione *(f)* alimentare *eentos-seekats-yohnay alee-mayn-tahray*
foot il piede *pee-e-day*; *(measure)* see **CONVERSION CHARTS**
football il calcio *kalcho*
for per *payr*
foreign straniero *stran-yero*
forest la foresta *fo-resta*
forget dimenticare *dee-mayntee-kahray*
fork la forchetta *forkayt-ta*; *(in road)* la biforcazione *beefor-kats-yohnay*
fortnight quindici giorni *kween-deechee jornee*
fountain la fontana *fon-tahna*
France la Francia *francha*
free *(not occupied)* libero *lee-bayro*; *(costing nothing)* gratis *gratees*
freezer il congelatore *konjay-la-tohray*
French francese *fran-chayzay*

French beans i fagiolini *fajo-leenee*
frequent frequente *fray-kwentay*
fresh fresco *fresko*
fridge il frigorifero *freego-ree-fayro*
fried fritto *freet-to*
friend l'amico/a *(m/f)* a-*meeko/a*
from da *da*
front davanti *da-vantee*
frozen *(food)* surgelato *soorjay-lahto*
fruit la frutta *froot-ta*
fruit juice il succo di frutta *sook-ko dee froot-ta*
fruit salad la macedonia *machay-don-ya*
frying-pan la padella *padel-la*
fuel il combustibile *komboo-stee-beelay*
fuel pump la pompa del carburante *pompa dayl karboo-rantay*
full pieno *pee-e-no*
full board la pensione completa *paynsee-ohnay komple-ta*
funny *(amusing)* divertente *deevayr-tentay*; *(strange)* strano *strahno*
fur la pelliccia *payl-leet-cha*
fuse il fusibile *foozee-beelay*

gallery la galleria *gal-layree-a*
gallon see **CONVERSION CHARTS**
gambling il gioco d'azzardo *joko dadz-zardo*
game il gioco *joko*
garage l'autorimessa *(f)* owto-reemays-sa*
garden il giardino *jar-deeno*
garlic l'aglio *(m)* al-yo*

gas il gas *gas*

gas cylinder la bombola di gas *bohm-bola dee gas*

gears le marce *mahrchay*

Genoa Genova *je-nova*

gentleman il signore *seen-yohray*

gents' la toilette (per uomini) *twalet (payr wo-meenee)*

genuine (leather, silver) vero *vayro*; (antique, picture) autentico *owten-teeko*

German tedesco *tay-daysko*

German measles la rosolia *rozo-leea*

Germany la Germania *jayrmahn-ya*

get (obtain) ottenere *ot-tay-nayray*; (receive) ricevere *reechay-vayray*; (fetch) prendere *pren-dayray*; **to get into** (house, clothes) entrare in *ayn-trahray een*; (vehicle) salire in *sa-leeray een*; **to get off** (bus etc) scendere da *shayn-dayray da*

gift il regalo *ray-gahlo*

gift shop il negozio di articoli da regalo *naygots-yo dee artee-kolee daray-gahlo*

gin il gin *gin*

ginger lo zenzero *dzaynd-zayro*

girl la ragazza *ragats-sa*

girlfriend la ragazza *ragats-sa*

give dare *dahray*; **to give back** restituire *raystee-too-eeray*

glass (for drinking) il bicchiere *beek-ye-ray*; (substance) il vetro *vaytro*

glasses gli occhiali *ok-yahlee*

gloves i guanti *gwantee*

glucose il glucosio *glookoz-yo*

glue la colla *kol-la*

go see GRAMMAR; **to go back** ritornare *reetor-nahray*; **to go down** (downstairs etc) scendere *shayn-dayray*; **to go in** entrare *ayn-trahray*; **to go out** (leave) uscire *oo-sheeray*

goggles gli occhiali *ok-yahlee*; (for skiing) gli occhiali da sci *ok-yahlee da shee*

gold d'oro *doroh*

golf il golf *golf*

golf course il campo di golf *kampo dee golf*

good buono *bwono*; (pleasant) bello *bel-lo*

good afternoon buona sera *bwona sayra*

goodbye arrivederci *ar-reevay-dayrchee*

good evening buona sera *bwona sayra*

good morning buon giorno *bwon jorno*

good night buona notte *bwona not-tay*

goose l'oca (f) *oka*

gramme il grammo *gram-mo*

grandfather il nonno *non-no*

grandmother la nonna *non-na*

grapefruit il pompelmo *pom-pelmo*

grapefruit juice il succo di pompelmo *sook-ko dee pom-pelmo*

grapes l'uva (f) *oova*

grass l'erba (f) *ayrba*

greasy grasso *gras-so*

green verde *vayrday*

green card la carta verde *karta vayrday*

grey grigio *greejo*

grilled alla griglia *al-la greel-ya*

grocer's il negozio di alimenti *naygots-yo dee alee-mayn-tahree*

ground la terra *ter-ra*

ground floor il pianterreno *peeanter-rayno*

groundsheet il telone impermeabile *tay-lohnay eempayr-may-ah-beelay*

group il gruppo *groop-po*

group passport il passaporto collettivo *pas-sa porto kol-layt-teevo*

guarantee la garanzia *(f) garant-see-a*

guard *(on train)* il capotreno *kapo-trayno*

guest *(house guest)* l'ospite *(m/f) os-peetay; (in hotel)* il/la cliente *klee-entay*

guesthouse la pensione familiare *paynsee-ohnay fameel-yahray*

guide[1] *n* la guida *gweeda*

guide[2] *vb* fare da guida *fahray da gweeda*

guidebook la guida *gweeda*

guided tour la visita guidata *veezeeta gwee-dahta*

gym shoes le scarpe da ginnastica *skarpay da jeen-nas-teeka*

haemorrhoids le emorroidi *aymorro-eedee*

hair i capelli *kapayl-lee*

hairbrush la spazzola per capelli *spats-sola payr kapayl-lee*

haircut il taglio di capelli *tal-yo dee kapayl-lee*

hairdresser *(male)* il parrucchiere *parrook-yeray; (female)* la parrucchiera *parrook-yera*

hairdryer il fôhn *fon*

hairgrip il fermacapelli *fayrma-kapayl-lee*

hair spray la lacca per capelli *lak-ka payr kapayl-lee*

half la metà *mayta; a half bottle of ...* una mezza bottiglia di ... *oona medz-za bot-teel-ya dee ...*

half board la mezza pensione *medz-za paynsee-ohnay*

half fare metà prezzo *mayta prets-so*

ham il prosciutto *proshoot-to*

hand la mano *mahno*

handbag la borsa *borsa*

handicapped handicappato *andee-kap-pahto*

handkerchief il fazzoletto *fats-solayt-to*

hand luggage il bagaglio a mano *bagal-yo a mahno*

hand-made fatto a mano *fat-to a mahno*

hangover i postumi d'una sbornia *po-stoomee doona zborn-ya*

happen succedere *soot-che-dayray; what happened?* cos'è successo? *ko-ze soot-ches-so*

happy felice *fay-leechay*

harbour il porto *porto*

hard duro *dooro*

hat il cappello *kap-pel-lo*

have *see* **GRAMMAR**

hay fever la febbre da fieno *feb-bray da fee-eno*

hazelnut la nocciola *not-chola*

he *see* GRAMMAR

head la testa *testa*

headache il mal di testa *mal dee testa*

head waiter il capocameriere *kapo-kamayr-yeray*

hear sentire *sayn-teeray*

heart il cuore *kworay*

heart attack l'infarto (m) *een-farto*

heater il termosifone *tayrmo-see-fohnay*

heating il riscaldamento *reeskal-da-maynto*

heavy pesante *pay-zantay*

hello ciao *chao*; *(on telephone)* pronto *prohnto*

help[1] *n* l'aiuto (m) *a-yootö*, **help!** aiuto! *a-yooto*

help[2] *vb* aiutare *a-yoo-tahray*; **can you help me?** può aiutarmi? *pwo a-yoo-tahrmee*

herb l'erba (f) aromatica *ayrba aro-mahtee-ka*

here qui *kwee*

high *(price, number, etc)* alto *alto*; *(speed)* forte *fortay*

high blood pressure la pressione alta *pray-see-ohnay alta*

high chair il seggiolone *sayd-jo-lohnay*

high tide l'alta marea (f) *alta ma-ray-a*

hill la collina *kol-leena*

hill walking l'escursionismo (m) *ayskoors-yo-neezmo*

hire noleggiare *nolayd-jahray*

hit colpire *kol-peeray*

hitchhike fare l'autostop *fahray low-to-stop*

hold tenere *tay-nayray*; *(contain)* contenere *kontay-nayray*

hold-up *(traffic jam)* l'ingorgo (m) *een-gorgo*

hole il buco *booko*

holiday la festa *festa*; **on holiday** in vacanza *een va-kantsa*

home la casa *kasa*

homesick: to be homesick avere nostalgia di casa *a-vayray nostal-jeea dee kasa*

honey il miele *mee-elay*

honeymoon la luna di miele *loona dee mee-elay*

hope sperare *spay-rahray*; **I hope so/not** spero di si/no *spayro dee see/no*

hors d'oeuvre l'antipasto (m) *antee-pasto*

horse il cavallo *kaval-lo*

hose il manicotto *manee-kot-to*

hospital l'ospedale (m) *ospay-dahlay*

hot caldo *kaldo*; **I'm hot** ho caldo *o kaldo*; **it's hot** *(weather)* fa caldo *fa kaldo*

hotel l'albergo (m) *al-bayrgo*

hour l'ora (f) *ohra*

house la casa *kasa*

house wine il vino della casa *veeno dayl-la kasa*

how *(in what way)* come *kohmay*; **how much?** quanto/a? *kwanto/a*; **how many?** quanti/e? *kwantee/ay*; **how are you?** come sta? *kohmay sta*

hungry: I am hungry ho fame *o fahmay*

hurry: I'm in a hurry ho fretta *o frayt-ta*

hurt fare male *fahray mahlay*; **my**

back hurts mi fa male la schiena *mee fa mahlay la skee-ena*

husband il marito *ma-reeto*

hydrofoil l'aliscafo *(m) alee-skahfo*

I *see* GRAMMAR

ice il ghiaccio *geeat-cho*

ice cream il gelato *jay-lahto*

iced *(drink)* ghiacciato *geeat-chahto*; *(coffee, tea)* freddo *frayd-do*

ice lolly il ghiacciolo *geeat-cholo*

ice rink la pista di pattinaggio su ghiaccio *peesta dee pat-teenad-jo soo geeat-cho*

if se *say*

ignition l'accensione *(f) at-chayns-yohnay*

ill malato *ma-lahto*

immediately subito *soo-beeto*

important importante *eempor-tantay*

impossible impossibile *eempos-see-beelay*

in in *een*

inch *see* CONVERSION CHARTS

included compreso *kom-prayzo*

indigestion la dispepsia *deespep-see-a*

indoors dentro *dayntro*; *(at home)* a casa *a kasa*

infectious contagioso *konta-johzo*

information le informazioni *eenfor-mats-yohnee*

information office l'ufficio *(m)* informazioni *oof-feecho eenfor-mats-yohnee*

injection l'iniezione *(f) een-yayts-yohnay*

injured ferito *fay-reeto*

ink l'inchiostro *(m) eenk-yostro*

insect l'insetto *(m) eenset-to*

insect bite la puntura d'insetto *poon-toora deenset-to*

insect repellent l'insettifugo *(m) eensayt-tee-foogo*

inside dentro *dayntro*

instant coffee il caffè solubile *kaf-fe soloo-beelay*

instead invece *een-vaychay*

instructor l'istruttore *(m) eestroot-tohray*

insulin l'insulina *(f) eensoo-leena*

insurance l'assicurazione *(f) as-seekoo-rats-yohnay*

insurance certificate il certificato di assicurazione *chayrtee-fee-kahto dee as-seekoo-rats-yohnay*

interesting interessante *eentay-ray-santay*

international internazionale *eentayr-nats-yo-nahlay*

interpreter l'interprete *(m/f) eentayr-praytay*

into in *een*

invitation l'invito *(m) een-veeto*

invite invitare *eenvee-tahray*

invoice la fattura *fat-toora*

Ireland l'Irlanda *(f) eer-landa*

Irish irlandese *eerlan-dayzay*

iron *(for clothes)* il ferro (da stiro) *ferro (da steero)*

ironmonger's il negozio di ferramenta *naygots-yo dee ferra-maynta*

is *see* GRAMMAR

island l'isola *(f) ee-zola*

it *see* GRAMMAR
Italian italiano *eetal-yahno*
Italy l'Italia *(f) eetal-ya*
itch il prurito *proo-reeto*

jack *(for car)* il cricco *kreek-ko*
jacket la giacca *jak-ka*
jam *(food)* la marmellata *mahrmayl-lahta*
jammed bloccato *blok-kahto*
jar *(container)* il vasetto *vazayt-to*
jazz il jazz *jazz*
jeans i jeans *jeans*
jelly *(dessert)* la gelatina *jayla-teena*
jellyfish la medusa *may-dooza*
jersey la maglia *mal-ya*
jeweller's la gioielleria *jo-yayl-lay-reea*
jewellery i gioielli *jo-yel-lee*
Jewish ebreo *ay-bre-o*
job il lavoro *la-vohro*
jog: to go jogging fare footing *fahray footing*
joke lo scherzo *skayrtso*
journey il viaggio *veead-jo*
jug la brocca *brok-ka*
juice il succo *sook-ko*
jump leads i cavi per far partire la macchina *kahve payr fahr parteeray la mak-keena*
junction *(road)* l'incrocio *(m) een-krohcho*
just: just two solamente due *sola-mayntay doo-ay*; **I've just arrived** sono appena arrivato *sohnoh ap-payna ar-ree-vahto*

keep *(retain)* tenere *tay-nayray*
kettle il bollitore *bo-lee-tohray*
key la chiave *kee-ahvay*
kidneys *(as food)* i rognoni *ron-yohnee*
kilo il chilo *keelo*
kilometre il chilometro *keelo-maytro*
kind¹ *n (sort, type)* il tipo *teepo*
kind² *adj (person)* gentile *jayn-teelay*
kiss baciare *ba-chahray*
kitchen la cucina *koo-cheena*
knife il coltello *koltel-lo*
know *(facts)* sapere *sa-payray*; **(be acquainted with)** conoscere *kono-shayray*; **I don't know** non lo so *non loh so*

lace *(of shoe)* il laccio *lat-cho*
ladder la scala *skahla*
ladies' toilette (per signore) *la twalet (payr seen-yohray)*
lady la signora *seen-yohra*
lager la birra bionda *beer-ra bee-onda*
lake il lago *lahgo*
lamb l'agnello *(m) an-yel-lo*
lamp la lampada *lam-pada*
lane la stradina *stra-deena*; **(of motorway)** la corsia *korsee-a*
language il linguaggio *leengwad-jo*; la lingua *leen-gwa*
large grande *granday*
last scorso *skorso*; **(final)** ultimo *ool-teemo*; **last week** la settimana scorsa *la sayt-tee-mahna skorsa*
late tardi *tardee*; **the train is late** il treno è in ritardo *eel trayno e een*

ree-**tardo**; **sorry we are late** scusi il ritardo skoozee eel ree-**tardo**

later più tardi pee-oo tardee

launderette la lavanderia automatica lavan-day**ree**-a owto-ma-teeka

laundry service il servizio di biancheria sayr**veets**-yo dee bee-ankay-**ree**-a

lavatory il gabinetto gabee-**nayt**-to

lawyer l'avvocato (m) av-vo-**kah**to

laxative il lassativo las-sa-**teevo**

layby la piazzola di sosta pee-ats-**sol**a dee sosta

lead (electric) il filo feelo

leader il capo kapo; (guide) la guida gweeda

leak (of gas, liquid) la perdita **payr**-deeta; (in roof) il buco booko

learn imparare eempa-**rah**ray

least: at least almeno al-**mayno**

leather il cuoio kwo-yo

leave (leave behind) lasciare lashahray; **when does the train leave?** quando parte il treno? kwando partay eel treno

leeks i porri por-ree

left: (on/to the) left a sinistra a see-neestra

left-luggage (office) il deposito bagagli daypo-zeeto ba**gal**-yee

leg la gamba gamba

lemon il limone lee-**moh**nay

lemonade la limonata leemo-**nah**ta

lemon tea il tè al limone te al lee-**moh**nay

lend prestare pray-**stah**ray

lens l'obiettivo (m) ob-yayt-**tee**vo

less meno mayno

lesson la lezione layts-**yoh**nay

let (allow) permettere payr**mayt**-tayray; (hire out) affittare af-feet-**tah**ray

letter la lettera **let**-tayra

lettuce la lattuga lat-**too**ga

library la biblioteca beeblee-o-**te**ka

licence il permesso payr**mes**-so

lid il coperchio ko**payrk**-yo

lie down sdraiarsi zdra-**yahr**see

lifeboat la scialuppa di salvataggio sha**loop**-pa dee salva-**tad**-jo

lifeguard il bagnino ban-**yee**no

life jacket il giubbotto salvagente joob-**bot**-to salva-**jen**tay

lift l'ascensore (m) ashayn-**soh**ray

lift pass (on ski slopes) la tessera per gli impianti di risalita **tes**-sayra payr lyee eempee-**ahn**-teedee reesa-**lee**ta

light la luce **loo**chay; **have you got a light?** ha da accendere? a da at-**chen**-dayray

light bulb la lampadina lampa-**dee**na

lighter l'accendino (m) at-chayn-**dee**no

like[1] prep come kohmay; **like you** come lei kohmay le-ee; **like this** cosi kozee

like[2] vb piacere pee-a-**chay**ray; **I like coffee** mi piace il caffè mee pee-achay eel kaffe

lime (fruit) la limetta leemayt-ta

line (row, queue) la fila **fee**la; (telephone) la linea **lee**nay-a

lip salve il burro di cacao boor-ro dee kaka-o

lipstick il rossetto *ros-sayt-to*

liqueur il liquore *lee-kwoh*ray

listen (to) ascoltare *askol-tahray*

litre il litro *leetro*

little: a little milk un po' di latte *oon po dee lat-tay*

live vivere *vee-vayray*; **I live in Edinburgh** abito ad Edimburgo *ah beeto ad aydeem-boorgo*

liver il fegato *fay-gato*

living room la sala *sahla*

loaf il pane *pahnay*

lobster l'aragosta *(f) ara-gosta*

local *(wine, speciality)* locale *lo-kahlay*

lock[1] *vb (door)* chiudere a chiave *keeoo day*ray *a kee-ahvay*

lock[2] *n (on door, box)* la serratura *sayr-ra-toora*

lollipop il lecca lecca *layk-ka layk ka*

London Londra *loh*ndra

long lungo *loongo*; **for a long time** molto tempo *mohlto tempo*

look guardare *gwar-dah*ray; **to look after** badare *ba-dah*ray; **to look for** cercare *chayr-kah*ray

lorry il camion *kam yon*

lose perdere *payr-dayray*

lost *(object)* perso *payrso*; **I have lost my wallet** ho perso il portafoglio *o payrso eel porta-fol-yo*; **I am lost** ho perso la strada *o payrso la strahda*

lost property office l'ufficio *(m)* oggetti smarriti *oof-feecho od-jet-tee zmar-reetee*

lot: a lot molto *mohlto*

lotion la lozione *lohts-yoh*nay

loud forte *fortay*

lounge *(in hotel)* il salone *sa-loh*nay

love *(person)* amare a *mahray*; **I love swimming** mi piace molto nuotare *mee pee achay* mohlto *nwo-tah*ray

lovely bellissimo *bayl-lees-seemo*

low basso *bas-so*; *(standard, quality)* scadente *ska-dentay*

low tide la bassa marea *has-sa ma-ray-a*

lucky fortunato *fortoo-nahto*

luggage i bagagli *bagal-yee*

luggage allowance il bagaglio permesso *bagal-yo payrmays-so*

luggage rack *(on car, in train)* il portabagagli *porta-hagal-yee*

luggage tag l'etichetta *(f) aytee-kayt-ta*

luggage trolley il carrello *kar-rel-lo*

lunch il pranzo *prantso*

luxury di lusso *dee loos-so*

macaroni i maccheroni *mak-kay-roh*nee

machine la macchina *mak-keena*

madam signora *seen-yoh*ra

magazine la rivista *ree-veesta*

maid *(in hotel)* la cameriera *kamayr-ye*ra

main principale *preenchee-pahlay*

main course il piatto principale *peeat-to preenchee-pah*lay

mains *(electric)* la linea principale *leenay-a preenchee-pah*lay

make *(generally)* fare *fahray*; *(meal)* preparare *praypa-rah*ray

make-up il trucco *trook-ko*

mallet la mazza *mats-sa*

man l'uomo *(m)* *womo*

manager il direttore *deerayt-tohray*

Mantua Mantova *man-tova*

many molti *mohltee*

map la carta *karta*

margarine la margarina *mahrga-reena*

mark *(stain)* la macchia *mak-ya*

market il mercato *mayr-kahto*

marmalade la marmellata di arance *marmayl-lahta dee a-ranchay*

married sposato *spo-zahto*

marzipan il marzapane *martsa-pahnay*

mascara il mascara *ma-skara*

mass *(in church)* la messa *mayss-sa*

matches i fiammiferi *fee-am-mee-fayree*

material *(cloth)* il tessuto *tays-sooto*

matter: it doesn't matter non importa *nohn eem-porta*; **what's the matter?** cosa c'è? *kosa che*

mayonnaise la maionese *ma-yo-nayzay*

meal il pasto *pasto*

mean *(signify)* voler dire *volayr deeray*; **what does this mean?** cosa vuol dire questo? *koza vwol deeray kwaysto*

meat la carne *karnay*

mechanic il meccanico *mayk-kaneeko*

medicine la medicina *maydee-cheena*

medium medio *med-yo*

medium rare poco cotto *poko kot-to*

meet incontrare *eenkon-trahray*

melon il melone *may-lohnay*

melt sciogliere *shol-yayray*

member *(of club etc)* il socio *socho*

men gli uomini *wo-meenee*

menu il menù *maynoo*

meringue la meringa *may-reenga*

message il messaggio *mays-sad-jo*

meter il contatore *konta-tohray*

metre il metro *metro*

migraine l'emicrania *(f)* *aymee-kran-ya*

Milan Milano *mee-lahno*

mile *see* **CONVERSION CHARTS**

milk il latte *laht-tay*

milkshake il frappé *frap-pay*

millimetre il millimetro *meel-lee-maytro*

million il milione *meel-yohnay*

mince la carne macinata *kahrnay machee-nahta*

mind: do you mind if I ...? Le dà fastidio se ...? *lay da fas-teed-yo say*

mineral water l'acqua *(f)* minerale *akwa meenay-rahlay*

minimum il minimo *mee-neemo*

minister *(church)* il sacerdote *sachayr-dotay*

minor road la strada secondaria *strahda saykon-dar-ya*

mint *(herb)* la menta *maynta*; *(sweet)* la mentina *mayn-teena*

minute il minuto *mee-nooto*

mirror lo specchio *spek-yo*

miss *(train etc)* perdere *payr-dayray*

Miss Signorina *seenyo-reena*

missing: my son is missing manca mio figlio *manka mee-o feel-yo*

mistake l'errore *(m)* ayr-**roh**ray

misty nebbioso *nayb-***yoh**zo

**misunderstanding: there's been a
misunderstanding** c'è stato un
malinteso *che stahto oon maleen-**tay**zo*

modern moderno *mo-***dayr**no

moisturizer l'idratante *(m)* eedra-**tan**tay

monastery il monastero *mona-**stay**ro*

money i soldi *soldee*

money order il vaglia *val-ya*

month il mese *mayzay*

monument il monumento *monoo-***mayn**to*

mop *(for floor)* il lavapavimenti *lahva-pavee-***mayn**tee*

more (than) più (di) *pee-oo (dee)*;
more wine please ancora un po' di
vino per favore *an-***ko**ra oon po dee
veeno payr fa-***voh**ray*

morning la mattina *mat-***tee**na

mosquito la zanzara *dzan-***dzah**ra

most: the most popular discotheque
la discoteca più frequentata *la
deeskoteka pee-oo fraykwayn-***tah**ta

mother la madre *mahdray*

motor il motore *mo-***toh**ray

motor boat il motoscafo *moto-***skah**fo

motor cycle la moto *mohto*

motorway l'autostrada *(f)* owto-**strah**da

mountain la montagna *montan-ya*

mousse la mousse *mousse*

mouth la bocca *bok-ka*

move: it isn't moving non si muove
nohn see mwovay

Mr Signor *seen-yohr*

Mrs Signora *seen-***yoh**ra

much molto *mohlto*; **it costs too
much** costa troppo *kohsta trop-po*

museum il museo *moozay o*

mushrooms i funghi *foongee*

music la musica **moo**-zeeka

mussel la cozza *kots-sa*

must dovere *do-***vay**ray

mustard la senape *se-napay*

mutton il montone *mon-***toh**nay

nail *(metal)* il chiodo *kee-odo*;
(fingernail) l'unghia *(f)* oong-ya

nail polish lo smalto per le unghie
zmalto payr lay oong-yay

nail polish remover l'acetone *(m)*
achay-**toh**nay

naked nudo *noodo*

name il nome *nohmay*

napkin il tovagliolo *toval-yolo*

Naples Napoli *nah polee*

nappies i pannolini per bambini
*pan-no-***lee**nee payr bam-***bee**nee

narrow stretto *strayt-to*

nationality la nazionalità *nats yona-***lee**ta

navy blue il blu marino *bloo ma-***ree**no

near vicino *vee-***chee**no

necessary necessario *naychays-***sar**yo

neck il collo *kol-lo*

necklace la collana *kol-***lah**na

need: I need ... ho bisogno di ...
o beezon-yo dee ...

needle l'ago *(m)* ahgo; **a needle and**

thread un ago e del filo *oon ahgo ay dayl feelo*

negative *(photography)* il negativo *nayga-teevo*

neighbour il vicino *vee-cheeno*

never mai *ma-ee*; **I never drink wine** non bevo mai il vino *nohn bayvo ma-ee eel veeno*

new nuovo *nwovo*

news le notizie *no-teets-yay*

newsagent il giornalaio *jorna-la-yo*

newspaper il giornale *jor-nahlay*

New Year l'Anno *(m)* Nuovo *an-no nwovo*

New Zealand la Nuova Zelanda *nwova dzay-landa*

next: the next stop la prossima fermata *la pros-seema fayr-mahta*; **next week** la settimana prossima *la sayt-tee-mahna pros-seema*

nice piacevole *pee-achay-volay*; *(person)* simpatico *seem-pahteeko*

night la notte *not-tay*; **at night** di notte *dee not-tay*

night club il night *night*

nightdress la camicia da notte *ka-meecha da not-tay*

no no *no*; **no thank you** no grazie *no grats-yay*

nobody nessuno *nays-soono*

noisy rumoroso *roomo-rohzo*

non-alcoholic analcolico *anal-ko-leeko*

none nessuno; **there's none left** non ce n'è più *nohn chay ne pee-oo*

non-smoking *(compartment)* per non-fumatori *payr nohn fooma-tohree*

north il nord *nord*

Northern Ireland L'Irlanda *(f)* del Nord *eer-landa dayl nord*

not non *nohn*

note *(bank note)* la banconota *banko-nota*; *(letter)* il biglietto *beel-yayt-to*

note pad il bloc-notes *blok-not*

nothing niente *nee-entay*

now adesso *ades-so*

number il numero *noo-mayro*

nurse l'infermiera *(f)* eenfayrm-yera*

nursery slope la pista pei principianti *peesta payr preencheep-yantee*

nut *(to eat)* la noce *nohchay*; *(for bolt)* il dado *dahdo*

occasionally ogni tanto *on-yee tanto*

of di *dee*

off *(machine etc)* spento *spento*; **this meat is off** questa carne è andata a male *kwasta karnay e an-dahta amahlay*

offer offrire *of-freeray*

office l'ufficio *(m)* oof-feecho*

often spesso *spes-so*

oil l'olio *(m)* ol-yo*

oil filter il filtro dell'olio *feeltro dayl-lol-yo*

ointment l'unguento *(m)* oon-gwento*

O.K. va bene *va benay*

old vecchio *vayk-yo*; **how old are you?** quanti anni ha? *kwantee an-nee a*

olive oil l'olio *(m)* d'oliva *ol-yo do-leeva*

olives le olive o-**lee**vay

omelette l'omelette (f) omay-**let**

on (light, engine) acceso at-**chay**zo; (tap) aperto a-**payr**to; **on the table** sulla tavola sool-la **tah**-vola

once una volta oona volta

one uno/una oono/oona

one-way (street) a senso unico a senso **oo**-neeko

onions le cipolle chee**pohl**-lay

only solo solo

open[1] adj aperto a-**payr**to

open[2] vb aprire a-**pree**ray

opera l'opera (f) o-**payra**

operator il/la centralinista chayntra-lee-**nee**sta

opposite: opposite the hotel di fronte all'albergo dee **fron**tay al-lal **bayr**go

or o oh

orange[1] adj arancione aran-**choh**nay

orange[2] n l'arancia (f) a-**ran**cha

orange juice il succo d'arancia sook-ko da-**ran**cha

order ordinare ordee-**nah**ray

oregano l'origano (m) o**ree**-gano

original originale oree-jee-**nah**lay

other: the other one l'altro laltro; **do you have any others?** ce ne sono altri? chay nay sohno altree

ounce see CONVERSION CHARTS

out (light) spento spento; **she's out** è fuori e **fwo**ree

outdoor (pool etc) all'aperto al-la-**payr**-to

outside fuori **fwo**ree

oven il forno forno

over (on top of) sopra sohpra

overcharge far pagare troppo far pa-**gah**ray trop-po

overnight (travel) di notte dee not-tay

owe dovere do-**vay**ray; **I owe you ...** le devo ... lay dayvo ...

owner il proprietario propree-ay**tar**-yo

oyster l'ostrica (f) os-**tree**ka

pack (luggage) fare le valigie fahray lay va-**lee**jay

package il pacco pak-ko

package tour il viaggio organizzato veead-jo orga-needz-zahto

packed lunch il cestino con il pranzo chay-**stee**no kohn eel prantso

packet il pacchetto pak-**kayt**-to

paddling pool la piscina per bambini pee-**shee**na payr bam-**bee**nee

Padua Padova **pah**-dova

paid pagato pa-**gah**to

painful doloroso dolo-**roh**zo

painkiller il calmante kal-**man**tay

painting il quadro kwadro

pair il paio pa-yo

palace il palazzo palats-so

pan la pentola **payn**-tola

pancake la crêpe krep

panties le mutandine mootan-**dee**nay

pants le mutande moo-**tan**day

paper la carta karta

paraffin il cherosene kayro-**ze**nay

parcel il pacco pak-ko

pardon *(I didn't understand)* scusi? *skoozee*; **I beg your pardon** mi scusi *mee skoozee*

parents i genitori *jaynee-**toh**ree*

park[1] *n* il parco *parko*

park[2] *vb* parcheggiare *parkayd-jahray*

parking disc il disco orario *deesko orar-yo*

parsley il prezzemolo *prayts-**se**molo*

part la parte *partay*

party *(group)* il gruppo *groop-po*

passenger il passeggero *pas-sayd-**jay**ro*

passport il passaporto *pas-sa-**por**to*

passport control il controllo passaporti *kon**trol**-lo pas-sa-**por**tee*

pasta la pasta *pasta*

pastry la pasta *pasta*; *(cake)* il pasticcino *pasteet-**chee**no*

pâté il pâté *patay*

path il sentiero *saynt-**ye**ro*

pay pagare *pa-**gah**ray*

payment il pagamento *paga-**mayn**to*

peaches le pesche *peskay*

peanuts le arachidi **ara**-*keedee*

pears le pere *payray*

peas i piselli *pee**zel**-lee*

peel *(fruit)* sbucciare *sboot-**chah**ray*

peg *(for clothes)* la molletta *mol-**layt**-ta*; *(for tent)* il picchetto *peek-**kayt**-to*

pen la penna *payn-na*

pencil la matita *ma-**tee**ta*

penicillin la penicillina *paynee-cheel-**lee**na*

penknife il temperino *taympay-**ree**no*

pensioner il pensionato *paynsee-o-**nah**to*

pepper *(spice)* il pepe *paypay*; *(vegetable)* il peperone *paypay-**roh**nay*

per: per hour all'ora *al-**lo**ra*; **per week** alla settimana *al-la sayt-tee-**mah**na*

perfect perfetto *payr**fayt**-to*

performance lo spettacolo *loh spayt-**tah**-kolo*

perfume il profumo *pro-**foo**mo*

perhaps forse *forsay*

period *(menstruation)* le mestruazioni *maystroo-ats-**yoh**nee*

perm la permanente *payrma-**nen**tay*

permit il permesso *payr**mes**-so*

person la persona *payr-**soh**na*

petrol la benzina *baynd-**zee**na*

petrol station la stazione di servizio *stats-**yoh**nay dee sayr**veets**-yo*

phone *see* **telephone**

photocopy fotocopiare *foto-kop-**yah**ray*

photograph la fotografia *foto-gra-**fee**-a*

picnic il picnic *peek**neek***

picture *(painting)* il quadro *kwadro*; *(photo)* la foto *foto*

pie la torta *torta*

piece il pezzo *pets-so*

pill la pillola *peel-lola*

pillow il guanciale *gwan-**chah**lay*

pillowcase la federa *fe-dayra*

pin lo spillo *speel-lo*

pineapple l'ananas *(m)* *a-nanas*

pink rosa *roza*

pint see **CONVERSION CHARTS; a pint of beer** una mezza birra *oona medz-za beer-ra*

pipe la pipa *peepa*

plane l'aereo *(m)* *a-e-ray-o*

plaster *(sticking plaster)* il cerotto *chayrot-to*

plastic di plastica *dee pla-steeka*

plate il piatto *pee-at-to*

platform il binario *beenar-yo*

play *(games)* giocare *jo-kahray*

playroom la stanza dei giochi *stantsa dayee jokee*

please per piacere *payr pee-a-chayray*; per favore *payr fa-vohray*

pleased contento *kon-tento*

plug *(electrical)* la spina *speena*; *(for sink)* il tappo *tap-po*

plum la susina *soo-seena*

plumber l'idraulico *(m)* *eedrow-leeko*

points *(in car)* le puntine *poon-teenay*

police la polizia *poleet-see-a*

policeman il poliziotto *poleets-yot-to*

police station il commissariato *kom-mees-sar-yahto*

polish *(for shoes)* il lucido *loo-cheedo*

polluted inquinato *eenkwee-nahto*

pony-trekking l'escursione *(f)* a cavallo *ayskoors-yohnay a kaval-lo*

pool *(swimming)* la piscina *peesheena*

popular popolare *popo-lahray*

Pope il papa *papa*

pork il maiale *ma-yahlay*

port *(seaport)* il porto *porto*; *(wine)* il porto *porto*

porter *(in hotel)* il portiere *port-yeray*; *(in station)* il facchino *fak-keeno*

possible possibile *pos-see-beelay*

post spedire *spay-deeray*

postbox la cassetta delle lettere *kas-sayt-ta dayl-lay let-tayray*

postcard la cartolina *karto leena*

postcode il codice postale *ko-deechay po stahlay*

post office l'ufficio *(m)* postale *oof-feecho po-stahlay*

pot *(for cooking)* la pentola *payn-tola*

potatoes le patate *pa-tahtay*

pottery la terracotta *tayr-rakot ta*

pound *(weight)* see **CONVERSION CHARTS**

pound *(money)* la sterlina *stayr-leena*

pram la carrozzina *kar rots-seena*

prawn il gambero *gam-bayro*

prefer preferire *prayfay-reeray*

pregnant incinta *een-cheenta*

prepare preparare *praypa-rahray*

prescription la ricetta *reechayt-ta*

present *(gift)* il regalo *ray-gahlo*

pretty carino *ka-reeno*

price il prezzo *prets-so*

priest il prete *pretay*

print *(photo)* la fotografia *foto-grafee-a*

private privato *pree-vahto*

probably probabilmente *proba-beel-mayntay*

problem il problema *pro-blema*

programme il programma *program-ma*

pronounce pronunciare *pronoon-chahray*; **how do you pronounce it?** come si pronuncia? *kohmay see pro-nooncha*

Protestant protestante *protay-stantay*

prunes le prugne *proon-yay*

public il pubblico *poob-bleeko*

public holiday la festa nazionale *festa nats-yo-nahlay*

pudding il dolce *dohlchay*

pull tirare *tee-rahray*

pullover il pullover *pullover*

puncture la foratura *fora-toora*

purple viola *vee-ola*

purse il borsellino *borsayl-leeno*

push spingere *speen-jayray*

put *(insert)* mettere *mayt-tayray*; *(put down)* posare *po-zahray*

pyjamas i pigiama *pee-jama*

queue la coda *koda*

quick veloce *vay-lohchay*

quickly velocemente *vaylo-chay-mayntay*

quiet *(place)* tranquillo *trankweel-lo*

quilt il piumino *pee-oo-meeno*

quite: it's quite good è abbastanza buono *e ab-bas-tantsa bwono*; **it's quite expensive** è piuttosto caro *e pee-oot-tosto kahro*

rabbit il coniglio *koneel-yo*

racket la racchetta *rak-kayt-ta*

radio la radio *rahd-yo*

radishes i ravanelli *rava-nayl-lee*

railway station la stazione *stats-yohnay*

rain la pioggia *peeod-ja*

raincoat l'impermeabile *(m) eempayr-may-ah-beelay*

raining: it's raining piove *pee-ovay*

raisin l'uvetta *(f) oovayt-ta*

rare *(unique)* raro *rahro*; *(steak)* al sangue *al sangwe*

raspberries i lamponi *lam-pohnee*

rate la tariffa *tareef-fa*; **rate of exchange** il cambio *kamb-yo*

raw crudo *kroodo*

razor il rasoio *razo-yo*

razor blades le lamette *lamayt-tay*

ready pronto *prohnto*

real vero *vayro*

receipt la ricevuta *reechay-voota*

recently recentemente *raychayn-tay-mayntay*

reception (desk) la reception *reception*

recipe la ricetta *reechet-ta*

recommend consigliare *konseel-yahray*

record *(music etc)* il disco *deesko*

red rosso *ros-so*

reduction la riduzione *reedoots-yohnay*

refill *(for pen)* il ricambio *reekamb-yo*; *(for lighter)* la bomboletta di gas *bombo-layt-ta dee gas*

refund il rimborso *reem-borso*

registered raccomandato *rak-koman-dahto*

regulations il regolamento *raygo-la-maynto*

reimburse rimborsare *reembor-sahray*

relation *(family)* il parente *pa-rentay*

relax rilassarsi *reelas-sahrsee*

reliable *(company, service)* sicuro *see-kooro*

remain restare *ray-stahray*

remember ricordare *reekor-dahray*

rent *(house)* affittare *af-feet-tahray*; *(car)* noleggiare *noled-jahray*

rental *(house)* l'affitto *(m) af-feet to*; *(car)* il nolo *nolo*

repair riparare *reepa rahray*

repeat ripetere *ree-petay-ray*

reservation la prenotazione *prayno-tats-yohnay*

reserve prenotare *prayno-tahray*

reserved prenotato *prayno tahto*

rest¹ *n (repose)* il riposo *ree-pozo*; **the rest of the wine** il resto del vino *eel resto dayl veeno*

rest² *vb* riposarsi *reepo-zahrsee*

restaurant il ristorante *reesto-rantay*

restaurant car il vagone ristorante *va gohnay reesto-rantay*

return *(go back)* ritornare *reetor-nahray*; *(give back)* restituire *raystee-too-eeray*

return ticket il biglietto di andata e ritorno *beelyayt-to dee an-dahta ay ree-torno*

reverse charge call la chiamata a carico del destinatario *kee-a-mahta a ka-reeko dayldaystee-na-tar-yo*

rheumatism il reumatismo *ray-ooma-teezmo*

rhubarb il rabarbaro *(m) rabar-baro*

rice il riso *reezo*

riding l'equitazione *(f) aykwee-tats-yohnay*; **to go riding** andare a cavallo *andah-ray a kaval-lo*

right¹ *adj (correct)* giusto *joosto*

right² *adv* : **(on/to the) right** a destra *a destra*

ring l'anello *(m) a-nel-lo*

ripe maturo *ma-tooro*

river il fiume *fee oomay*

road la strada *strahda*

road map la carta stradale *karta stra-dahlay*

roast arrosto *ar-rosto*

roll *(bread)* il panino *pa-neeno*

Rome Roma *rohma*

roof il tetto *tayt-to*

roof-rack il portabagagli *porta-bagal-yee*

room *(in house, hotel)* la stanza *stantsa*; *(space)* lo spazio *spats-yo*

room service il servizio da camera *sayrveets-yo da ka-mayra*

rope il cavo *kahvo*

rosé rosato *ro-zahto*

rough *(sea)* mosso *mos-so*

round rotondo *ro-tohndo*; **round the corner** dietro l'angolo *dee-etro lan-golo*

route l'itinerario *(m) eetee-nayrar-yo*

rowing boat la barca a remi *barka a raymee*

rubber la gomma *gohm-ma*

rubber band l'elastico *(m) aylas-teeko*

rubbish la spazzatura *spats-sa-toora*

rucksack lo zaino *dza-eeno*

ruins le rovine *ro-veenay*

rum il rum *room*

run *(skiing)* la pista *peesta*
rush hour l'ora *(f)* di punta *ohra dee poonta*

safe[1] *n* la cassaforte *kas-sa-fortay*
safe[2] *adj (beach, medicine)* non pericoloso *non payree-ko-loh-zo*
safety pin la spilla di sicurezza *speel-la dee seekoo-rayts-sa*
sail la vela *vayla*
sailboard la tavola per il surf *tah-vola payr eel surf*
sailing *(sport)* la vela *vayla*
salad l'insalata *(f)* mista *eensa-lahta meesta*
salad dressing il condimento per l'insalata *kondee-maynto payr leensa-lahta*
salmon il salmone *sal-mohnay*
salt il sale *sahlay*
same stesso *stays-so*
sand la sabbia *sab-ya*
sandals i sandali *san-dalee*
sandwich il panino *pa-neeno*
sanitary towels gli assorbenti *as-sor-bayntee*
sardine la sardina *sar-deena*
Sardinia Sardegna *sardayn-ya*
sauce la salsa *salsa*
saucepan la pentola *payn-tola*
saucer il piattino *peeat-teeno*
sauna la sauna *sa-oona*
sausage la salsiccia *salseet-cha*
savoury *(not sweet)* salato *sa-lahto*
say dire *deeray*
scallop il pettine *pet-teenay*
scampi gli scampi *skampee*

scarf la sciarpa *shahrpa*
school la scuola *skwola*
scissors le forbici *forbee-chee*
scotch lo scotch *skotch*
Scotland la Scozia *skots-ya*
Scottish scozzese *skots-sayzay*
screw la vite *veetay*
screwdriver il cacciavite *kat-cha-veetay*
sculpture *(object)* la scultura *skool-toora*
sea il mare *mahray*
seafood I frutti di mare *froot-tee dee mahray*
seasickness il mal di mare *mahl dee mahray*
seaside: at the seaside al mare *al mahray*
season ticket l'abbonamento *(m)* ab-bona-maynto*
seat *(chair)* la sedia *sed-ya; (in train, theatre)* il posto *pohstoh*
second *adj* secondo *say-kohndo*
second class la seconda classe *say-kohnda klas-say*
see vedere *vay-dayray*
self-service self-service *self service*
sell vendere *ven-dayray*
Sellotape ® lo scotch *skotch*
send mandare *man-dahray; spedire spay-deeray*
senior citizen l'anziano/a *(m/f) ants-yahno/a*
separate separato *saypa-rahto*
serious grave *grahvay*
serve servire *sayr-veeray*
service *(in restaurant)* il servizio *sayrveets-yo*

service charge il servizio *sayrveets-yo*

set menu il menù turistico *maynoo tooree-steeko*

shade l'ombra *(f) ohmbra*

shallow poco profondo *poko profohndo*

shampoo lo shampoo *shampo*

shampoo and set shampoo e messa in piega *shampo ay may-sa een pee-ega*

shandy la birra con gassosa *beer-ra kohn gas-sohza*

share dividere *deevee-dayray*

shave farsi la barba *farsee la barba*

shaving cream la crema da barba *krema da barba*

she see GRAMMAR

sheet il lenzuolo *laynt-swolo*

shellfish i frutti di mare *froot-tee dee mahray*

sherry lo sherry *sherry*

ship la nave *nahvay*

shirt la camicia *ka-meecha*

shock absorber l'ammortizzatore *(m) am-morteedz-za-tohray*

shoe la scarpa *skarpa*

shop il negozio *naygots-yo*

shopping: to go shopping fare compere *fahray kom-payray*

short corto *korto*

short cut la scorciatoia *skorcha-to-ya*

shorts i calzoncini corti *kaltson-cheenee kortee*

show[1] *n* lo spettacolo *spayt-tah-kolo*

show[2] *vb* mostrare *mo-strahray*

shower la doccia *dot-cha*

shrimp il gamberetto *gambay-rayt-to*

Sicily Sicilia *seecheel-ya*

sick *(ill)* malato *ma-lahto*

sightseeing il turismo *too-reezmo*

sign il segnale *sayn-yahlay*

signature la firma *feerma*

silk la seta *seta*

silver argento *ar-jaynto*

similar simile *see-meelay*

simple semplice *saym-pleechay*

single *(unmarried)* non sposato *nohn spo-zahto, (not double)* singolo *seen-golo; (ticket)* di (solo) andata *dee (sohlo) an-dahta*

single bed il letto a una piazza *letto a oona pee-ats-sa*

single room la camera singola *kamayra seen-gola*

sink il lavandino *lavan-deeno*

sir signore *seen-yohray*

sister la sorella *sorel-la*

sit: please, sit down prego, si accomodi *praygo see ak-komoh-dee*

size la misura *mee-zoora*

skate il pattino *pat-teeno*

skating il pattinaggio *pat-teen-adjo*

ski[1] *vb* sciare *shee-ahray*

ski[2] *n* lo sci *shee*

ski boots gli scarponi da sci *skar-pohnee da shee*

skiing lo sci *shee*

skimmed milk il latte scremato *laht-tay skray-mahto*

skin la pelle *pel-lay*

skindiving le attività subacquee *at-teevee-ta soobak-way-ay*

ski pants i pantaloni da sci *panta-lohnee da shee*

ski pass la tessera per gli impianti di risalita *tes-sayra payr lee eempee-**ahn**-tee dee reesa-**lee**ta*

ski pole la racchetta da sci *rak-**kayt**-ta da shee*

skirt la gonna *gon-na*

ski run la pista *peesta*

ski suit il completo da sci *kom-**pleto** da shee*

sledge la slitta *zleet-ta*

sleep dormire *dor-**mee**ray*

sleeper *(in train)* la cuccetta *koot-**chayt**-ta*

sleeping bag il sacco a pelo *sak-ko a paylo*

sleeping car il vagone letto *va-**goh**nay let-to*

sleeping pill il sonnifero *son-**nee**-fayro*

slice la fetta *fet-ta*

slide *(photograph)* la diapositiva *dee-a-pozee-**tee**va*

slippers le pantofole *panto-**folay***

slow lento *laynto*

small piccolo *peek-kolo*

smaller (than) più piccolo (di) *pee-oo **peek**-kolo (dee)*

smell *(pleasant)* il profumo *pro-**foo**mo; (unpleasant)* il puzzo *poots-so*

smoke[1] *n* il fumo *foomo*

smoke[2] *vb* fumare *foo-**mah**ray*

smoked affumicato *af-foomee-**kah**to*

snack bar la tavola calda ***tah**-vola kalda*

snorkel il boccaglio *bok-**kal**-lyo*

snow la neve *nayvay*

snowed up isolato a causa della neve *eezo-**lah**to a **kow**za dayl-la nayvay*

snowing: it's snowing nevica ***nay**-veeka*

so: so much tanto *tanto*

soap la saponetta *sapo-**nayt**-ta*

soap powder il detersivo *daytayr-**see**vo*

sober sobrio *sobree-o*

socket la presa *prayza*

socks i calzini *kalt-**see**nee*

soda la soda *soda*

soft soffice ***sof**-feechay*

soft drink l'analcolico *(m) anal-**ko**-leekoh*

some del/della *dayl/dayl-la; (plural)* alcuni/alcune *al-**koo**nee/al-**koo**nay*

someone qualcuno *kwal-**koo**no*

something qualcosa *kwal-**ko**sa*

sometimes qualche volta *kwalkay volta*

son il figlio *feel-yo*

song la canzone *kant-**soh**nay*

soon presto *presto*

sore: my back is sore mi fa male la schiena *mee fa mahlay la skee-**e**na*

sorry: I'm sorry! mi scusi! *mee skoozee*

sort: what sort of cheese? che tipo di formaggio? *kay teepo dee for**mad**-jo*

soup la minestra *mee-**ne**stra*

south il sud *sood*

souvenir il souvenir *soovneer*

space: parking space il posto *pohstoh*

spade la paletta *pa**layt**-ta*

spanner la chiave *kee-**ah**vay*

WORDS

spare wheel la ruota di scorta *rwota dee skorta*

spark plug la candela *kan-dayla*

sparkling frizzante *freets-santay*

speak parlare *par-lahray*

special speciale *spay-chahlay*

speciality la specialità *spaycha-leeta*

speed la velocità *vaylo-cheeta*

speed limit il limite di velocità *lee-meetay dee vaylo-cheeta*

spell: how do you spell it? come si scrive? *komay see skreevay*

spicy piccante *peek-kantay*

spinach gli spinaci *spee-nachee*

spirits i liquori *lee-kwohree*

sponge la spugna *spoon-ya*

spoon il cucchiaio *kook-ya-yo*

sport lo sport *sport*

spring (season) la primavera *preema-ve-ra*

square (in town) la piazza *pee-ats-sa*

squash (game) lo squash *squash*; (drink) la spremuta *spray-moota*

stairs le scale *skahlay*

stalls (theatre) la platea *platay-a*

stamp il trancobollo *franko-bohl-lo*

start cominciare *komeen-chahray*

starter (in meal) l'antipasto (m) *antee-pasto*; (in car) il motorino d'avviamento *moto-reeno dav-vee-a-maynto*

station la stazione *stats-yohnay*

stationer's la cartoleria *karto-lay-reea*

stay (remain) restare *ray-stahray*; **I'm staying at a hotel** sto in un albergo *sto een oon al-bayrgo*

steak la bistecca *beestayk-ka*

steep ripido *ree-peedo*

sterling la sterlina *stayr-leena*

stew lo stufato *stoo-fahto*

steward lo steward *steward*

stewardess la hostess *hostess*

sticking plaster il cerotto *chayrot-to*

still (motionless) fermo *fayrmo*

sting la puntura *poon-toora*

stockings le calze *kaltsay*

stomach la pancia *pancha*

stomach upset il mal di pancia *mal dee pancha*

stop fermarsi *fayr-mahrsee*

stopover la sosta *sosta*

storm la tempesta *taym-pesta*

straight on diritto *deereet-to*

straw (for drinking) la cannuccia *kan-noot-cha*

strawberries le fragole *frahgolay*

street la strada *strahda*

street map la piantina *pee-an-teena*

string lo spago *spahgo*

striped a strisce *a streeshay*

strong forte *fortay*

stuck bloccato *blok-kahto*

student (male) lo studente *stoo-dayntay*; (female) la studentessa *stoodayn-tes-sa*

stung punto *poonto*

stupid stupido *stoo-peedo*

suddenly improvvisamente *eempro-veeza-mayntay*

suede il camoscio *ka-mosho*

sugar lo zucchero *tsook-kayro*

suit (man's) l'abito (m) *a-beeto*; (women's) il tailleur *ta-yer*

suitcase la valigia *va-leeja*

summer l'estate *(f) ay-stah*tay

sun il sole *sohlay*

sunbathe prendere il sole ***prayn-**dayray eel sohlay*

sunburn la scottatura solare *skot-ta-toora so-lah*ray

sunglasses gli occhiali da sole *ok-yahlee da sohlay*

sunny assolato *as-so-lah*to; **it's sunny** c'è il sole *che eel sohlay*

sunshade l'ombrellone *(m) ombrayl-loh*nay

sunstroke l'insolazione *(f) eenso-lats-**yoh**nay*

suntan lotion la lozione solare *lohts-yoh*nay *so-lah*ray

supermarket il supermercato *soopayr-mayr-**kah**to*

supper *(dinner)* la cena *chayna*

supplement il supplemento *soop-play-**mayn**to*

sure sicuro *see-koo*ro

surface mail la posta ordinaria *posta ordee-**nar**-ya*

surfboard la tavola per surfing ***tah**-vola payr surfing*

surfing surfing *surfing*

surname il cognome *kon-yoh*may

suspension la sospensione *sospayn-see-**oh**nay*

sweater il maglione *mal-**yoh**nay*

sweet dolce *dohl*chay

sweetener il dolcificante *dohl-cheefee-**kan**tay*

sweets le caramelle *kara-**mel**-lay*

swim nuotare *nwo-**tah**ray*

swimming pool la piscina *pee-**shee**na*

swimsuit il costume da bagno *ko-stoo*may *da ban-yo*

Swiss svizzero ***zveet**-sayro*

switch l'interruttore *(m) eentayr-root-**toh**ray*

switch off spegnere ***spen**-yayray*

switch on accendere *at-**chen**-dayray*

Switzerland la Svizzera ***zveet**-sayra*

synagogue la sinagoga *seena-goga*

table la tavola ***tah**-vola*

tablecloth la tovaglia *toval-ya*

tablespoon il cucchiaio *kook-**ya**-yo*

tablet la pastiglia *pasteel-ya*

table tennis il ping-pong *peeng pong*

take *(carry)* portare *por-**tah**ray*; *(grab, seize)* prendere ***pren**-dayray*; **how long does it take?** quanto tempo ci vuole? *kwanto tempo chee vwolay*

talc il borotalco *boro-**tal**ko*

talk parlare *par-**lah**ray*

tall alto *alto*

tampons i tamponi *tam-**poh**nee*

tap il rubinetto *roobee-**nayt**-to*

tape il nastro *nastro*

tape-recorder il registratore *rayjee-stra-**toh**ray*

tartar sauce la salsa tartara *salsa tar-tara*

taste[1] *vb* : **can I taste some?** ne posso assaggiare un po'? *nay pos-so as-sad-**jay**ray un po*

taste[2] *n* il sapore *sa-**poh**ray*

tax la tassa *tas-sa*

taxi il taxi *taksee*

taxi rank il posteggio dei taxi *postayd-jo day-ee taksee*

tea il tè *te*

tea bag la bustina di tè *boo-steena dee te*

teach insegnare *eensayn-yahray*

teacher l'insegnante *(m/f)* *eensayn-yantay*

teapot la teiera *tay-yera*

teaspoon il cucchiaino *kook-ya-eeno*

teat la tettarella *tayt-tarel-la*

teeshirt la maglietta *mal-yayt-la*

teeth i denti *dentee*

telegram il telegramma *taylay-gramma*

telephone il telefono *tayle-fono*

telephone box la cabina telefonica *ka-beena taylay-fo-neeka*

telephone call la telefonata *taylay-fo-nahta*

telephone directory l'elenco *(m)* telefonico *ay-lenko taylay-fo-neeko*

television la televisione *taylay-veez-yohnay*

television set il televisore *taylay-vee-zohray*

telex il telex *telex*

tell dire *deeray*

temperature la temperatura *taympay-ra-toora*; **to have a temperature** avere la febbre *a-vayray la feb-bray*

temporary temporaneo *taympo-rahnay-o*

tennis il tennis *ten-nees*

tennis court il campo da tennis *kampo da ten-nees*

tennis racket la racchetta da tennis *rak-kayt-ta da ten-nees*

tent la tenda *tenda*

tent peg il picchetto *peekayt-to*

terminus *(for buses)* il capolinea *kapo-leenay-a*; *(station)* la stazione di testa *stats-yohnay dee testa*

terrace la terrazza *tayr-rats-sa*

thank you grazie *grats-yay*; **thank you very much** tante grazie *tantay grats-yay*

that quel/quella *kwayl/kwayl-la*; **that one** quello là *kwayl-lo la*

thaw: it's thawing sta sgelando *sta zjay-lando*

theatre il teatro *tay-atro*

then: they will be away then a quell'epoca saranno via *a kwayl-le-poka sarah-no vee-a*

there li *lee*; **there is/there are** c'è/ci sono *che/chee sohno*

thermometer il termometro *tayrmo-maytro*

these questi/queste *kwaystee/ kwaystay*

they *see* GRAMMAR

thief il ladro *lahdro*

thing la cosa *kosa*; **my things** la mia roba *la mee-a roba*

think pensare *payn-sahray*

third terzo *tayrtso*

thirsty: I'm thirsty ho sete *o saytay*

this questo/questa *kwaysto/kwaysta*; **this one** questo qui *kwaysto kwee*

those quelli/quelle *kwayl lee/ kwayl-lay*

thread il filo *feelo*

throat la gola *gohla*

throat lozenges le pastiglie per la gola *pasteel-yay payr la gohla*

through attraverso *at-tra-vayrso*

thunderstorm il temporale *taympo-rahlay*

ticket il biglietto *beel-yayt-to*

ticket collector il controllore *kontro-lohray*

ticket office la biglietteria *beel-yayt-tayree-a*

tide la marea *maray-a*

tie la cravatta *kravat-ta*

tights i collant *kol-lant*

till[1] *n* la cassa *kas-sa*

till[2] *prep* fino a *feeno a*

time il tempo *tempo*; **this time** questa volta *kwaysta volta*

timetable board il tabellone degli orari *tabayl-lohnay dayl-lyee o-rahree*

tin la scatola *skah-tola*

tinfoil la carta stagnola *karta stan-yola*

tin-opener l'apriscatole *(m) apree-skah-tolay*

tip *(to waiter etc)* la mancia *mancha*

tipped con filtro *kohn feeltro*

tired stanco *stanko*

tissues i fazzoletti di carta *fats-so-layt-tee dee karta*

to a *ah*; **to London** a Londra *a lohndra*; **to Spain** in Spagna *een span-ya*

toast il pane tostato *pahnay to-stahto*

tobacco il tabacco *tabak-ko*

tobacconist il tabaccaio *tabak-ka-yo*

today oggi *od-jee*

together insieme *een-see-emay*

toilet la toilette *twalet*

toilet paper la carta igienica *karta ee-je-neeka*

toll il pedaggio *paydad-jo*

tomato il pomodoro *pomo-doro*

tomato juice il succo di pomodoro *sook-ko dee pomo-doro*

tomorrow domani *do-mahnee*

tongue la lingua *leengwa*

tonic water l'acqua *(f)* tonica *akwa to-neeka*

tonight stasera *sta-sayra*

too *(also)* anche *ankay*; **it's too big** è troppo grande *e trop-po granday*

tooth il dente *dentay*

toothache: I have toothache ho mal di denti *o mal dee dentee*

toothbrush lo spazzolino da denti *spats-solee-no da dentee*

toothpaste il dentifricio *dayntee-freecho*

top[1] *adj* : **the top floor** l'ultimo piano *lool-teemo pee-ahno*

top[2] *n* la cima *cheema*; **on top of ...** sopra... *sohpra...*

torch la pila *peela*

torn strappato *strap-pahto*

total il totale *to-tahlay*

tough *(meat)* duro *dooro*

tour il giro *jeero*

tourist il turista *too-reesta*

tourist office l'ufficio *(m)* informazioni turistiche *oof-feecho eenfor-mats-yohnee tooree-steekay*

tourist ticket il biglietto turistico *beel-yayt-to tooree-steeko*

tow rimorchiare *reemork-yahray*

towel l'asciugamano *(m) ashoo-ga-mahno*

town la città *cheet-ta*
town centre il centro *chentro*
town plan la pianta della città *pee-anta dayl-la cheet-ta*
tow rope il cavo da rimorchio *kahvo da reemork-yo*
toy il giocattolo *jokat-tolo*
traditional tradizionale *tradeets-yo-nahlay*
traffic il traffico *traf-feeko*
trailer il rimorchio *reemork-yo*
train il treno *treno*
tram il tram *tram*
translate tradurre *tradoor-ray*
translation la traduzione *tradoots-yohnay*
travel viaggiare *vee-ad-jahray*
travel agent l'agente *(m)* di viaggio *a jentay dee vee-ad-jo*
traveller's cheques i travellers *travellers*
tray il vassoio *vas-so-yo*
tree l'albero *(m) al-bayro*
trim la spuntata *spoon-tahta*
trip la gita *jeeta*
trouble la difficoltà *deef-fee-kolta*
trousers i pantaloni *panta-lohnee*
true vero *vayro*
trunk *(luggage)* il baule *ba-oolay*
trunks i calzoncini da bagno *kaltson-cheenee da ban-yo*
try provare *pro-vahray*
try on provare *pro-vahray*
T-shirt la maglietta *mal-yayt-ta*
tuna il tonno *ton-no*
tunnel la galleria *gal-lay-ree-a*
Turin Torino *to-reeno*

turkey il tacchino *tak-keeno*
turn *(handle, wheel)* girare *jee-rahray*
turnip la rapa *rahpa*
turn off *(light, etc)* spegnere *spayn-yayray; (tap)* chiudere *kee-oo-dayray*
turn on *(light etc)* accendere *at-chen-dayray; (tap)* aprire *a-preeray*
tweezers le pinzette *peentsayt-tay*
twice due volte *doo-ay voltay*
twin-bedded room la camera con letti gemelli *ka mayra kohn let-tee jaymel-lee*
typical tipico *tee-peeko*
tyre la gomma *gohm-ma*
tyre pressure la pressione delle gomme *prays-yohnay dayl-lay gohm-may*

umbrella l'ombrello *(m) ombrel-lo*
uncomfortable scomodo *sko-modo*
unconscious svenuto *zvay-nooto*
under sotto *sohto-to*
underground la metropolitana *maytro-polee-tahna*
underpass il sottopassaggio *sot-topas-sad-jo*
understand capire *ka-peeray*; **I don't understand** non capisco *nohn ka peesko*
underwear la biancheria intima *bee-ankay-ree-a een-teema*
United States gli Stati Uniti *stahtee oo-neetee*
university l'università *(f) oonee-vayrsee-ta*
unpack: I have to unpack devo disfare le valigie *dayvo dees-fahray lay va-leejay*

up su *soo*; **up there** lassù *las-soo*
upstairs di sopra *dee sohpra*
urgent urgente *oor-jentay*
USA USA *oosa*
use usare *oo-zahray*
useful utile *oo-teelay*
usual solito *so-leeto*
usually di solito *dee so-leeto*

vacancies *(in hotel)* le stanze libere *stantsay lee-bayray*
vacuum cleaner l'aspirapolvere *(m) aspee-rapohl-vayray*
valid valido *va-leedo*
valley la valle *val-lay*
valuable di valore *dee va-lohray*
valuables i valori *va-lohree*
van il furgone *foor-gohnay*
vase il vaso *vahzo*
VAT l'IVA *(f) eeva*
veal il vitello *veetayl-lo*
vegetables le verdure *vayr-dooray*
vegetarian il vegetariano *vayjay-tar-yahno*
Venice Venezia *vaynayts-ya*
ventilator il ventilatore *vayntee-la-tohray*
vermouth il vermut *vayrmoot*
very molto *mohlto*
vest la canottiera *kanot-tyera*
via via *vee-a*
video il video *vee-dayo*
view la vista *veesta*
villa la villa *veel-la*
village il paese *pa-ayzay*
vinegar l'aceto *(m) a-chayto*
vineyard la vigna *veen-ya*

visa il visto *veesto*
visit visitare *veezee-tahray*
vitamin la vitamina *veeta-meena*
vodka la vodka *vodka*
voltage il voltaggio *voltad-jo*

waist la cintura *cheen-toora*
wait (for) aspettare *aspayt-tahray*
waiter il cameriere *kamayr-ye-ray*
waiting room la sala d'aspetto *sahla daspet-to*
waitress la cameriera *kamayr-ye-ra*
wake up svegliarsi *svayl-yarsee*
Wales il Galles *gal-lays*
walk¹ *vb* andare a piedi *an-dahray a pee-e-dee*
walk² *n* : **to go for a walk** fare una passeggiata *fahray oona pas-sayd-jahta*
wallet il portafoglio *porta-fol-yo*
walnut la noce *nochay*
want volere *vo-layray*
warm caldo *kaldo*
warning triangle il triangolo *tree-angolo*
wash lavare *la-vahray*; **to wash oneself** lavarsi *la-varsee*
washbasin il lavabo *la-vahbo*
washing machine la lavatrice *lava-treechay*
washing powder il detersivo *daytayr-seevo*
washing-up liquid il detersivo per i piatti *daytayr-seevo payr ee pee-attee*
wasp la vespa *vespa*
waste bin il bidone della spazzatura *bee-dohnay dayl-la spats-atoo-ra*

watch[1] n l'orologio (m) oro-**lo**jo

watch[2] vb (look at) guardare

water l'acqua (f) akwa

waterfall la cascata kas-**kah**ta

water heater lo scaldabagno skalda-**ban**-yo

watermelon l'anguria (f) angoo-**ree**a

waterproof impermeabile eempayr-may-**ah**-beelay

water skiing lo sci acquatico shee akwa-teeko

wave (on sea) l'onda onda

wax la cera chayra

way (manner) il modo modo; (route) la strada strahda; **this way** di qua dee kwa

we see GRAMMAR

weak (person) debole day-bolay; (coffee) leggero led-**je**ro

wear portare por-**tah**ray

weather il tempo tempo

wedding il matrimonio matree-**mon**-yo

week la settimana sayt-tee-**mah**na

weekday il giorno feriale jorno fayr-**yah**lay

weekend il week-end weekend

weekly rate la tariffa settimanale ta**reef** fa sayt-teema-**nah**lay

weight il peso payso

welcome benvenuto baynvay-**noo**to

well bene benay; **he's not well** non sta bene nohn sta benay; **well done** (steak) ben cotto ben kot-to

Welsh gallese gal-**lay**zay

west ovest ovest

wet bagnato ban-**yah**to

wetsuit la muta moota

what che kay; **what is it?** cos'è? koze

wheel la ruota rwota

wheelchair la sedia a rotelle sed-ya a rotel-lay

when quando kwando

where dove dovay

which quale kwale; **which is it?** qual'è? kwah**le**

while mentre mayntray; **in a while** fra poco fra poko

whipped montato mon-**tah**to

whisky il whisky whisky

white bianco bee-**an**ko

who: who is it? chi è? kee e

whole tutto toot-to

wholemeal integrale eentay-**grah**lay

whose: whose is it? di chi è? dee kee e

why perché payrkay

wide largo largo

wife la moglie mol-yay

window la finestra fee-**nes**tra; (shop) la vetrina vay-**tree**na

windscreen il parabrezza para-**braydz**-za

windsurfing il windsurf windsurf

windy: it's windy c'è vento che vento

wine il vino veeno

wine list la lista dei vini leesta dayee veenee

winter l'inverno (m) een-**vayr**no

with con kohn

without senza sentsa

woman la donna don-na

wood (material) il legno layn-yo; (forest) il bosco bosko

wool la lana lana

word la parola *pa-rola*

work *(person)* lavorare *lavo-rahray*; *(machine, car)* funzionare *foontsyo-nahray*

worried preoccupato *pray-ok-koo-pahto*

worse peggio *ped-jo*

worth: it's worth £100 vale cento sterline *vahlay chento stayr-leenay*

wrap (up) incartare *eenkar-tahray*

wrapping paper la carta da pacchi *karta da pak-kee*

write scrivere *skree-vayray*

writing paper la carta da lettera *karta da let-tayra*

wrong sbagliato *sbal-yahto*; **sorry, wrong number** scusi, ho sbagliato numero *skoozee o zbal-yahto noo-mayro*

yacht lo yacht *yacht*

year l'anno *(m)* an-no

yellow giallo *jal-lo*

yes si *see*; **yes please** si, grazie *see gratsyay*

yesterday ieri *yeree*

yet: not yet non ancora *non an-kora*

yoghurt lo yogurt *yogurt*

you *see* GRAMMAR

young giovane *joh-vanay*

youth hostel l'ostello *(m)* della gioventù *ostel-lo dayl-la jovayn-too*

zero lo zero *dzero*

zip la cerniera *chayrn-ye-ra*

zoo lo zoo *dzo-oh*

a at; in; to

abbacchio *m* baby lamb

abbaglianti *mpl* : **accendere gli abbaglianti** to put one's headlights on full beam

abbastanza enough; quite

abbazia *f* abbey

abbigliamento *m* clothes; **abbigliamento intimo** underwear; **abbigliamento sportivo** casual wear; **abbigliamento uomo/donna/bambino** men's/ladies'/children's wear

abboccato(a) semi-sweet *(wine)*

abbonamento *m* subscription; season ticket

abbonato(a) *m/f* subscriber; season ticket holder

abbronzante *m* suntan oil/cream

abbronzatura *f* suntan

abitante *m/f* inhabitant

abito *m* dress; suit *(man's)*; **abito da sera** evening dress *(woman's)*

abuso *m* : **ogni abuso sarà punito** penalty for improper use

accamparsi to camp

accanto nearby; **accanto a** beside

accendere to turn on; to light; **accendere i fari** switch on your headlights; **vietato accendere fuochi** do not light a fire

accensione *f* ignition; **l'accensione della luce rossa segnala il fuori servizio** machine not in use when red light shows

acceso(a) on

accesso *m* access; fit; **divieto di accesso** no entry; **divieto di accesso ai non addetti ai lavori** authorized personnel only

accessori *mpl* accessories

accettare to accept; **non si accettano assegni** we do not accept cheques

accettazione *f* acceptance; reception; check-in; **accettazione bagagli** check-in

acciuga *f* anchovy

accomodarsi to make oneself comfortable; **si accomodi** do sit down

accompagnatore *m* escort; **accompagnatore turistico** courier

acconciature *fpl* hairdresser's (shop)

acconto *m* down payment

accostare **accostare (a)** to bring near (to); to draw up (at); **accostare la banconota a destra** place the banknote on the right

aceto *m* vinegar; **aceto di vino** wine vinegar

ACI *m* ~ A.A.

acqua *f* water; **acqua corrente** running water; **acqua minerale** mineral water; **acqua potabile** drinking water; **acqua tonica** tonic water

acquisto *m* purchase

acuto(a) sharp; acute

addebitare to debit

addetto(a): **personale addetto** relevant staff

aereo *m* plane; aircraft

aeroplano *m* aeroplane

aeroporto *m* airport

aeroportuale: **formalità aeroportuali** *fpl* airport formalities

affare *m* : **per affari** on business

affettato *m* (sliced) cold meat

affissione *f* : **divieto di affissione** post no bills

affittanze *fpl* : **vendite affittanze** property for sale or rent

affittare to rent; to let

affittasi to let

affitto *m* lease; rent; hire; **affitto ombrelloni** beach umbrellas for hire

affogato(a) drowned; poached (*egg*)

affrancare to stamp (*letter*)

affresco *m* fresco

affumicato(a) smoked

agente *m* : **agente verificatore** ticket inspector; **agente di viaggi** travel agent; **agenti portuali** port inspectors

agenzia *f* agency; **agenzia di navigazione** shipping agency; **agenzia di viaggi** travel agency; **agenzia viaggiatori Ferrovie dello Stato** rail travel agency

agitare to shake

aglio *m* garlic

agnello *m* lamb; **agnello arrosto** roast lamb

agnolotti *mpl* squares or circles of pasta with meat filling

agosto *m* August

agrodolce: **in agrodolce** in a sweet and sour sauce

aiuola *f* flowerbed; **è vietato calpestare le aiuole** keep off the grass

aiuto! *m* help!

albergatore *m* hotelier

albergo *m* hotel

albero *m* tree; mast; **alberi in banchina** overhanging trees

albicocca *f* apricot

alcolici *mpl* liquor

alcolico(a) alcoholic (*drink*)

alcuni(e) some

alcuno(a) any

aliante *m* glider

alici: **filetti di alici** *mpl* anchovy fillets

alimentari *mpl* : **negozio di alimentari** grocer's (shop)

aliscafo *m* hydrofoil

allacciare to fasten; **allacciare la cintura di sicurezza** to fasten one's seat belt

allappante slightly tart (*wine*)

allarme *m* alarm; **allarme antincendio** fire alarm

allergia *f* allergy

allestimento *m* : **mostra/vetrina in allestimento** exhibition/window display in preparation

alloggio *m* lodgings; accommodation

Alpi *fpl* Alps

alpinismo *m* mountaineering

alt: **alt dogana/polizia** stop: customs/police

alto high; aloud

alto(a) high; tall; **alta stagione** high season

altopiano *m* plateau

altro(a) other; **altre direzioni** other destinations

alzare to raise; to turn up

alzarsi to get up; to stand up; to

rise

amabile sweet *(wine)*

amaro(a) bitter

amarognolo(a) slightly bitter

ambasciata *f* embassy

ambiente *m* environment

ambulanza *f* ambulance

ambulatorio *m* consulting room; **ambulatorio comunale** health centre

America *f* America

ammandorlato(a): vino ammandorlato wine with a flavour of almonds

ammirare to admire

ammobigliato furnished

ammontare a to amount to

ammorbidente *m* softener

ammortizzatore *m* shock absorber

amo *m* (fish) hook

ampio(a) loose; wide; full-bodied *(wine)*

analcolico(a) non-alcoholic; soft *(drink)*

ananas *m* pineapple

anatra *f* duck; **anatra arrosto** roast duck; **anatra in agrodolce** duck in sweet and sour sauce

anche too; also; even

ancora[1] still; yet; again; **ancora del formaggio** more cheese

ancora[2] *f* anchor

andare to go; **andiamo** let's go

anello *m* : **anello di fondo** cross-country skiing circuit

anfiteatro *m* amphitheatre

angolo *m* corner; angle

anguilla *f* eel; **anguilla in umido** eel stew

anguria *f* watermelon

animatore *m* organizer; compère

animazione *f*: **programma di animazione** organized entertainment

animelle *fpl* sweetbreads

annata *f* vintage; year; **vino d'annata** vintage wine

anno *m* year; **quanti anni ha?** how old are you?

annullamento *m* cancellation; **spese per l'annullamento del servizio** cancellation fee

annuncio *m* announcement; advertisement

anteprima *f* preview

antiappannante *m* demister

antichità *f* antique; antiquity

anticipo *m* advance *(loan)*; **in anticipo** in advance; early

anticoncezionale *m* contraceptive

anticongelante *m* antifreeze

antigelo *m* antifreeze; de-icer

antincendio: bombola antincendio *f* fire extinguisher

antipasto *m* hors d'oeuvre; **antipasto misto** mixed hors d'oeuvre, usually containing cured hams and pickles; **antipasto di pesce** fish hors d'oeuvre; **antipasto di frutti di mare** seafood hors d'oeuvre

antiquario *m* antique dealer

antisettico *m* antiseptic

ape *f* bee

aperitivo *m* aperitif

aperto(a) open; on; **all'aperto** in the open (air); open-air

apparecchio *m* appliance; **apparecchi pubblici** public telephones

appartamento *m* flat; apartment

appetito *m* appetite; **buon appetito!** enjoy your meal!

appoggiarsi: è pericoloso appoggiarsi do not lean against the door(s)

appuntamento *m* appointment; date

aprile *m* April

aprire to open; to turn on; **non aprire prima che il treno sia fermo** do not open while the train is in motion

arachide *f* peanut

aragosta *f* lobster

arancia *f* orange

aranciata *f* orangeade

arancino *m* rice croquette stuffed with meat

archeologico(a): museo archeologico archaeological museum

architettura *f* architecture

arco *m* arch; bow *(for arrow, violin)*

area *f* area; **area di parcheggio** parking area; **area di servizio** service area

argento *m* silver

argilla *f* clay

aria *f* air; tune; **con aria condizionata** air-conditioned

aringa *f* herring

arista *f* chine of pork

armadietto *m* locker

armadio *m* cupboard; wardrobe

armi *fpl* arms *(weapons)*

aromi *mpl* seasoning; herbs

arredato(a): appartamento arredato furnished flat

arrivare to arrive

arrivederci goodbye

arrivo *m* arrival; **arrivi/partenze nazionali** domestic arrivals/ departures; **arrivi/partenze internazionali** international arrivals/departures

arrosto roast; roast meat; **arrosto di manzo/tacchino/vitello** roast beef/turkey/veal

arte *f* art; craft

articolo *m* article; **articoli da pesca** fishing equipment; **articoli da spiaggia** beachwear and accessories; **articoli sportivi** sports goods

artigiano *m* craftsman

ascensore *m* lift

asciugamano *m* towel

asciugatoio *m* hair-drier

asparagi *mpl* asparagus

aspettare to wait; to wait for; to expect

aspro(a) sharp; sour

assaggiare to taste

assegno *m* cheque; allowance *(state payment)*

assente absent

assicurazione *f* insurance; **assicurazione contro terzi** third party insurance; **assicurazione casco** comprehensive insurance

assistente *m/f* assistant; **assistente sanitario** health worker

assistenza *f* assistance; **assistenza qualificata** expert service; **assistenza sanitaria** health service

associazione *f* society; association; **associazione turistica giovanile** tourist association for young people

assorbente: assorbente igienico *m* sanitary towel

assortito(a) assorted

asta *f* auction

Asti town in Piedmont famous for its red, white and sparkling white wines

astice *m* lobster

ATG *abbrev. of* **associazione turistica giovanile**

atlante *m* atlas

Atlantico *m* Atlantic Ocean

ATM public transport service

attendere to wait for

attenti al cane beware of the dog

attenzione *f* attention; **attenzione allo scalino** mind the step; **attenzione alla corrente elettrica** danger: electricity

atterraggio *m* landing (of plane); **atterraggio di emergenza** emergency landing; **atterraggio di fortuna** crash-landing

atterrare to land (plane)

attestare: si attesta che ... it is hereby declared that ...

attestazione *f*: **attestazione di versamento** proof of payment

attività *f* activity; **attività sportive** sporting activities

attracco *m* berthing; berth; **divieto di attracco a imbarcazioni non autorizzate** berths for authorized craft only

attraversamento pedonale *m* pedestrian crossing

attraversare to cross; **vietato attraversare i binari** do not cross the track

attraverso through

attrazione *f* attraction

attrezzatura *f* equipment

auguri *mpl*: **tanti auguri** all the best

austriaco(a) Austrian

autentico(a) genuine

autista *m* driver; chauffeur

autobus *m* bus

autocorriera *f* country bus

autocorsa *f* bus

autoforniture *fpl* car parts and accessories

automobilista *m/f* motorist

autonoleggio *m* car hire; **autonoleggio con autista** chauffeur-drive service

autopompa *f* fire engine

autopullman *m* bus; coach

autorimessa *f* garage (for parking)

autoritratto *m* self-portrait

autorizzazione *f* authorization; **autorizzazione scritta** written authorization

autostop *m* hitchhiking

autostrada *f* motorway; **autostrada a pedaggio** toll road

autovettura *f* motor car

avanti in front; forward(s)

avena *f* oats

avere to have

avvenuto(a): l'avvenuta accettazione è indicata da un segnale acustico an acoustic signal indicates that your money has been accepted

avvertire to warn

avvisare to inform; to warn

avviso m warning; announcement; advertisement; notice; **avviso alla clientela** notice to customers

azienda f : **azienda turismo** local tourist board; **azienda di soggiorno** local tourist board

azzurro(a) blue

baccalà m dried salted cod; **baccalà alla vicentina** salt cod cooked in milk with white wine, spices, anchovies, onion and garlic

bagagliaio m boot (of car); luggage van

bagaglio m luggage; **bagaglio a mano** hand luggage; **bagaglio personale** personal luggage

bagnarsi to get wet; to bathe

bagnino m lifeguard

bagno m bathroom; bath; **bagni** bathing establishment

baia f bay

balcone m balcony

balletto m ballet

balneazione f : **è proibita la balneazione** bathing strictly prohibited

balsamo m hair conditioner

bambinaia f nurse(maid)

bambino(a) m/f child; baby

banca f bank

banchina f platform; quay; quayside; **banchina cedevole** soft verge

banco m counter; bench; **banco di registrazione** check-in (desk); **banco di sabbia** sandbank

barbabietola f beetroot

Barbaresco m dry, full-bodied red wine from Piedmont

Barbera m dry, full-bodied, deep-red wine from Piedmont

barbiere m barber

barbo m barbel

barca f boat

Bardolino m light, dry red wine from the area around Verona

barista m/f barman; barmaid

Barolo m dry, full-bodied red wine with a taste of violets, from Piedmont

base f : **pranzo a base di pesce/carne** lunch with fish/meat as the main course

bastare to be enough

bastoncini mpl : **bastoncini di merluzzo** cod fish fingers; **bastoncini di pesce** fish fingers

battello m boat; **battello da diporto** pleasure boat; **battello di salvataggio** lifeboat

batteria f battery (in car)

battistero m baptistry

beccaccia f woodcock

beccaccino m snipe

bello(a) beautiful; handsome; lovely; fine

Bel Paese m soft, mild creamy cheese

bene well; all right; **va bene** okay;

it's okay

beneficiario *m* payee

benvenuto(a) welcome

benzina *f* petrol

berlina *f* saloon *(car)*

bersaglio *m* target

bevanda *f* drink

biancheria *f* linen *(for beds, table)*; **biancheria casa** household linens; **biancheria intima** underwear

bianco(a) white; blank; **lasciate in bianco per favore** please leave blank; **pesce/carne in bianco** boiled fish/meat

bibita *f* soft drink

biblioteca *f* library; bookcase

bicchiere *m* glass

bicicletta *f* bicycle

bigiotteria *f* costume jewellery

bigliettaio *m* bus conductor

biglietteria *f* ticket office; **biglietteria aerea** air travel ticket office

biglietto *m* note; ticket; card; **biglietto di andata e ritorno** return ticket; **biglietto di solo andata** single ticket; **biglietto orario** ticket valid for one hour from time of issue; **il biglietto deve essere convalidato all'inizio del viaggio** tickets must be punched at start of journey and kept ready for inspection

bignè *m* cream puff

bin. *abbrev. of* **binario**

binario *m* track; line; platform

birra *f* beer; **birra alla spina** draught beer; **birra chiara** lager; **birra piccola/grande** half pint/pint of beer; **birre estere** foreign beers;

birre nazionali Italian beers

birreria *f* brewery; type of pub

biscotto *m* biscuit

bisogno *m* need; **avere bisogno di** to need

bistecca *f* steak; **bistecca ai ferri** grilled steak; **bistecca di filetto** fillet steak; **bistecca alla fiorentina** T-bone steak

bivio *m* fork

blocchetto *m*: **biglietti in blocchetti** books of tickets

blocco *m* block; notepad; **per evitare il blocco dell'ascensore ...** to prevent the lift from jamming ...

boa *f* buoy

bocce *fpl* bowls *(game)*

bocconcini *mpl* rolls of veal with ham and cheese filling

bolla *f* bubble; blister

bollito *m* boiled meat; **bollito misto** assorted boiled meats

bombolone *m* doughnut

bordo: salire a bordo to go aboard; **a bordo della nave** aboard ship

borgo *m* district

borsa *f* handbag; bag; briefcase; **la Borsa** the stock market; the stock exchange; **borsa nera** black market

bosco *m* wood *(forest)*

bottega *f* shop

botteghino *m* box office

bovino(a): carni bovine *fpl* beef

braciola *f* chop; **braciola di maiale** pork chop

brandina *f* camp-bed

branzino *m* bass

brasato *m* braised beef

britannico(a) British

brocca f jug

broccoletti mpl broccoli

brodetto m : **brodetto di pesce** spicy fish soup

brodo m stock; **riso/pasta in brodo** rice/noodle soup

bruciore di stomaco heartburn

brutto(a) ugly

buca f hole; **buca per le lettere** letter box

bucato m washing; laundry; **per bucato in lavatrice** for machine washing; **per bucato a mano** for hand washing

budino m pudding

buongustaio m gourmet

buono m voucher; coupon; token

buono(a) good; **buon giorno!** good morning/afternoon!; **buona sera!** good evening!; **buona notte!** good night!; **a buon mercato** cheap

burrasca f storm

burro m butter

bustina f sachet; **bustina di tè** tea bag

cabina f cabin; beach hut; cubicle; **cabina interna/esterna** cabin below/above deck; **cabina telefonica** telephone booth; **cabina doppia/tripla/quadrupla** two-/three-/four-berth cabin

cacao m cocoa; **cacao amaro** cocoa with no added sugar

caccia f hunting; shooting

cacciagione f game (hunting)

cacciatora: alla cacciatora with tomatoes, mushrooms, shallots, ham and wine

cacciucco m : **cacciucco alla livornese** spiced fish soup with garlic and sage

caciocavallo m firm cheese made from cow's or sheep's milk

caduta f fall; **caduta massi/sassi** danger, falling rocks/stones

caffè m café; coffee; **caffè corretto** coffee containing a liqueur; **caffè decaffeinato** decaffeinated coffee; **caffè in grani** coffee beans; **caffè lungo** weak black coffee; **caffè macchiato** coffee with a dash of milk; **caffè macinato** ground coffee; **caffè nero** black coffee; **caffè ristretto** extra-strong black coffee; **caffè tostato** roasted coffee

caffellatte m white coffee

calamaretti ripieni mpl stuffed baby squid

calamari mpl : **calamari fritti** fried squid

calcio m football (game)

caldarroste fpl roast chestnuts

caldo(a) warm; hot

calendario m : **calendario partenze** departure dates

calmante m painkiller

calzature fpl shoeshop

calzoleria f shoeshop

calzone m savoury turnover made with pizza dough, usually filled with cheese and ham

cambiare to change; to exchange

cambio m change; exchange; rate of exchange; gears; **cambio di asciugamani/delle lenzuola** change of towels/sheets; **cambio filtri** oil filter change; **cambio olio rapido** quick oil change; **cambio medio applicato** average rate of exchange applied; **cambio valute** exchange office

camera f room; **camera (da letto)** bedroom; **camera libera** vacancy; **camera matrimoniale** double room; **camera singola** single room

cameriere m waiter

camerini prova mpl fitting rooms

camiceria f shirt shop

camion m lorry

camionabile for heavy vehicles

campagna f country; countryside; campaign

campana f bell

campanello m bell; doorbell

campeggio m camping; camp(ing) site; **campeggio libero** free camp site

campo m field; **campo da gioco** playing field; **campo di golf** golf course; **campo sportivo** sports ground; **campo da tennis** tennis court

camposanto m cemetery

canale m canal; channel

cancellare to rub out; to cancel

cancelleria f stationery

cancello m gate

candeggina f bleach

candela candle; spark plug

cane m dog

canna da pesca f fishing rod

cannella f cinnamon

cannelloni mpl tubes of pasta stuffed with sauce and baked

cannolo m cream horn

cannone m gun; cannon

canocchia f squill

cantante m/f singer

cantiere m building site; **cantiere navale** shipyard

cantina f cellar; wine cellar

canzone f song

capelli mpl hair; **capelli grassi/secchi** greasy/dry hair

capitaneria f: **capitaneria (di porto)** port authorities

capitello m capital

capo m head; leader; boss; **capo di vestiario** item of clothing; **detersivo per capi delicati** soap powder for delicates

Capodanno m New Year's Day

capogruppo m group leader

capolavoro m masterpiece

capolinea m terminus

capoluogo m ≈ county town

caponata f a dish containing aubergines, onions, celery, peppers, tomatoes, olives, and garlic

capotreno m guard (on train)

cappella f chapel

cappuccino m frothy white coffee

capriolo m roe deer

carabiniere m (military) policeman

caraffa f decanter; carafe

caramella f sweet

carburante m fuel; **pompa del carburante** fuel pump

carciofo m artichoke; **carciofi alla romana** stuffed artichokes, sautéed

caricare to charge (battery)

carico *m* : accesso consentito per operazioni di carico e scarico access for loading and unloading only

carne *f* meat; flesh; **carne di cervo** venison; **carne di maiale** pork; **carne di manzo** beef; **carne di montone** mutton; **carne tritata** mince; **carni bianche** white meats; **carni nere** game meats; **carni rosse** red meats

caro(a) dear

carota *f* carrot

carpa *f* carp

carpaccio *m* thin slices of raw beef with oil, salt and pepper and sometimes grated cheese

carpione *m* : **pesce in carpione** soused fish

carreggiata doppia *f* dual carriageway

carrello *m* trolley; **carrello per bagagli** luggage trolley

carro *m* cart; **carro attrezzi** breakdown van

carrozza *f* : **carrozza ferroviaria** railway carriage; **carrozze cuccette** carriages with couchettes; **carrozze letto** sleepers

carrozzeria *f* bodywork; body repairer's

carta *f* paper; card; **alla carta** à la carte; **Carta d'Argento** Senior Citizen's rail card; **carta di credito** credit card; **Carta Famiglia** Family rail card; **carta geografica** map (of country); **carta d'identità** identity card; **carta igienica** toilet paper; **carta d'imbarco** boarding pass; **carta nautica** chart (map); **carta**

stradale road map; **carta verde** green card

cartello *m* sign; signpost; cartel

cartoccio *m* paper bag; **pesce/pollo al cartoccio** fish/chicken baked in tinfoil

cartoleria *f* stationer's (shop)

cartolina *f* postcard; greetings card

casa *f* house; home; **offerto(a) dalla casa** on the house; **casa colonica** farmhouse

casalinghi *mpl* household articles

cascata *f* waterfall

casco *m* helmet; crash helmet

casella postale *f* post-office box

casello *m* : **casello autostradale** motorway tollgate

caserma *f* barracks; **caserma dei pompieri** fire station

caso *m* : **in caso di necessità rompere il vetro** in an emergency break the glass

cassa *f* cash desk; cash register; crate; **cassa chiusa** position closed; **cassa continua** night safe

cassaforte *f* strongbox; safe

cassata *f* tutti-frutti ice cream

casseruola *f* casserole (dish)

cassiere(a) *m/f* cashier; teller

castagna *f* chestnut

castagnaccio *m* chestnut cake with pine nuts and sultanas

castello *m* castle

catena *f* chain; range (of mountains); **catene (da neve)** snow chains; **obbligo di catene** snow chains compulsory

cattedrale *f* cathedral

cattivo(a) bad; nasty; evil; naughty

causa *f* : **a causa di** because of

cauzione *f* security (for loan); deposit (for key etc.)

cavallo *m* horse

caviale *m* caviar(e)

cavolfiore *m* cauliflower

cavolini di Bruxelles *mpl* Brussels sprouts

cavolo *m* cabbage; **cavolo cappuccio** spring cabbage; **cavolo rapa** kohlrabi

c'è there is

cedro *m* cedar; lime (fruit)

C.E.E. *f* E.E.C.

cefalo *m* grey mullet

cena *f* dinner; supper; dinner party

cenone *m* : **cenone di Capodanno** New Year's Eve dinner

cento hundred

centralino *m* switchboard

centro *m* centre; **centro assistenza tecnica** after-sales department; **centro città** city centre; town centre; **centro commerciale** shopping centre

ceramica *f* pottery

cernia *f* : **cernia (gigante)** grouper; **cernia (di fondo)** stone bass

cervella *fpl* brains (food)

cervello *m* brain; brains (as food)

cervo *m* deer; **carne di cervo** venison

cestino *m* waste paper basket

cetriolino *m* gherkin

cetriolo *m* cucumber

che that; than; which; who(m); what

chi who; whom

chiamarsi: come si chiama? what's your name?

chiamata *f* call; **chiamata urbana/interurbana** local/long-distance call

Chianti *m* dry red/white wine from Tuscany

chiaretto *m* claret

chiaro(a) clear; light (bright, pale)

chiave *f* key; spanner

chiedere to ask; to ask for

chiesa *f* church

chilometraggio *m* ≈ mileage; **chilometraggio illimitato** unlimited mileage

chilometrico(a): biglietto chilometrico special ticket which can be used to travel a certain number of kilometres

chinotto *m* bitter orange drink

chiodo *m* : **chiodo di garofano** clove

chiudere to shut; to close; to turn off

chiudersi to shut; to close; **si chiude da sé** door closes automatically

chiuso(a) shut; off (tap, light etc.)

chiusura *f* : **(orario di) chiusura** closing time

ci there; **ci sono** there are

cialda *f* waffle

ciao hello; goodbye

ciclomotore *m* moped

cicoria *f* endive; chicory

cielo *m* sky

ciliegia *f* cherry

cima *f* peak; top; **cima alla genovese** cold veal stuffed with sausage, eggs and mushrooms

cimitero m cemetery

cincín cheers!

cinghia f belt; **cinghia della ventola** fan belt

cinghiale m wild boar

cinquanta fifty

cinque five

Cinqueterre sweet or dry white wines from Liguria

cintura f belt (for waist); **cintura di sicurezza** seat belt; **cintura di salvataggio** lifebelt

ciò this; that

cioccolata f chocolate; **cioccolata calda** hot chocolate

cioccolatini mpl chocolates

cioccolato m chocolate; **cioccolato al latte/fondente** milk/plain chocolate

cipolla f onion

cipollina f spring onion

circolare to move (traffic)

circolazione f : **valido per la circolazione all'estero** valid for driving abroad

circonvallazione f ring road; bypass

CIT f Italian Tourist Agency

citofono m intercom

città f town; city

classe f class; **classe economica** economy class; **classe turistica** tourist class

cliente m/f customer; guest (at hotel); **cliente successivo** next customer

clima m climate

climatizzato(a) air-conditioned

cocco m coconut

cocomero m watermelon

coda f : **coda di rospo** angler fish

cognome m surname; **cognome da nubile** maiden name

coincidenza f connection (train etc); **coincidenze nazionali/ internazionali** domestic/ international connections

colazione f breakfast; **colazione all'inglese** English breakfast

collant m tights

collegamento m : **collegamenti internazionali** international connections

collo m : **colli a mano** hand luggage

colonna f column

combustibile m fuel

come like; as; how; **come?** pardon?; **com'è?** what's it like?; **come va?** how are you?

comitiva f group; **sconti per comitive** discounts for group bookings

commesso(a) m/f assistant; clerk

commissariato m police station

comodità fpl amenities

comodo(a) comfortable

compagnia f company; **compagnia aerea** airline; **compagnia di navigazione** shipping company

complesso(a) complex; **complesso (pop)** pop group

completo(a) complete; full up (bus etc); **al completo** full; no vacancies

comporre to dial (number)

compreso(a) including; **servizio**

compreso inclusive of service; **... non compreso(a)** exclusive of ...

comune *m* town council; town hall; municipality

comunicazione *f*: **comunicazione telefonica** telephone call; **ottenere la comunicazione** to get through (*on phone*)

con with

concessionario *m* agent; dealer

conciliare: conciliare una contravvenzione to settle a fine on the spot

condimento *m* dressing; seasoning

condizionamento dell'aria *m* air-conditioning

condizioni *fpl* terms (*of contract*); **condizioni del tempo permettendo** weather permitting

condomino *m*: **riservato ai condomini** residents only

conducente *m* driver (*of taxi, bus*)

confermare to confirm

confezione *f*: **confezioni per signora** ladies' wear; **confezioni da uomo** menswear

confine *m* boundary; border

coniglio *m* rabbit; **coniglio stufato** rabbit stew

cono *m*: **cono gelato** ice-cream cone

consegna *f* delivery; consignment

conservante *m*: **senza conservanti** no preservatives

conservare: conservare in luogo fresco e asciutto store in a cool, dry place

conservarsi: da conservarsi in frigo keep refrigerated

conservatorio *m* academy of music

conservazione *f*: **a lunga conservazione** UHT

consiglio *m* advice; **consigli per l'uso** instructions for use

consolato *m* consulate

consumarsi: da consumarsi entro il ... best before ...

consumazione *f* drink; **buono per una consumazione** voucher for one drink; **la consumazione è obbligatoria** customers only, please

contante *m* cash; **pagare in contanti** to pay cash

contatore *m* meter

contattare to contact

contatto *m* contact; **mettersi in contatto con** to contact

contento happy

continuare to continue

conto *m* bill; account

contorno *m* vegetables

contratto *m* contract; **contratto di viaggio** travel agreement terms

contravvenzione *f* fine

contro against; versus

controllo *m* check; control; **controllo gomme** tyre check; **controllo passaporti** passport control

controllore *m* ticket inspector

convalidare to punch; to stamp; **convalida punch** (or stamp) this side; **convalidare il biglietto qui** please punch your ticket here; **il biglietto va convalidato nell' obliteratrice all'inizio del viaggio** insert your ticket in the machine at the start of your journey

convocazione f : **area convocazione gruppi** group rendezvous point

coperto m place setting; cover charge; **al coperto** indoor (games)

copertura f cover (insurance)

coppa[1] f : **coppa dell'olio** sump (in car); **coppa gelato** dish of ice cream; tub of ice cream

coppa[2] f large pork sausage

corposo(a) full-bodied

corrente f power (electricity); current

corridolo m corridor

corsa f race; journey; **corsa semplice** single fare; **ultima corsa** last bus; **corse ippiche** horse-racing

corsetteria f corsetry

corsia f lane; ward (in hospital); **corsia di emergenza** hard shoulder; **corsia di sorpasso** outside lane

corso m course; **corso dei cambi** exchange rates; **corso intensivo** crash course; **corso di lingua** language course

cortile m courtyard; yard; playground

cosa f thing

coscia f : **coscia di pollo** chicken leg

cosciotto m : **cosciotto d'agnello** leg of lamb

così so; thus (in this way)

costa f coast

Costa Azzurra f French Riviera

costare to cost

costata f : **costata di manzo** beef entrecôte

costo m cost

costola f rib

costoletta f cutlet; **costoletta di vitello alla milanese** veal cutlet coated in breadcrumbs and fried

costume m costume; fancy dress; **costume da bagno** swimsuit; swimming trunks

cotechino m spiced pork sausage

cotoletta f cutlet; **cotoletta alla milanese** chop/cutlet coated in breadcrumbs and fried

cotto(a) done (cooked); **poco cotto(a)** underdone

cozza f mussel; **cozze alla marinara** breaded mussels cooked in wine with herbs, carrot and onion

crauti mpl sauerkraut

credito m credit; **non si fa credito** no credit given; **credito residuo** credit remaining

crema f cream; custard; **crema per barba** shaving cream; **crema per calzature** shoe cream; **crema fredda ai cetrioli** cucumber with yoghurt, milk, cream and parsley; **crema per le mani** hand cream; **crema con pomodori** cream of tomato soup; **crema solare** sun cream; **crema per il viso** face cream

crescione m cress

crespella f fried pastry twist

croccante f crisp

crocchetta f croquette; **crocchette di patate** potato croquettes

crocevia m crossroads

crociera f cruise; **crociera d'altura** sea cruise

crollo m : **pericolo di crollo** danger: building unsafe

cronaca f news

crostacei mpl shellfish

crostino m crouton; canapé

crudo(a) raw (uncooked)

cubetto di ghiaccio m ice cube

cuccetta f couchette; berth

cucchiaino m teaspoon

cucchiaio m spoon; dessertspoon

cucina f kitchen; cooker; cooking

cucinino m kitchenette; **cucinino accessoriato** fully-equipped kitchenette; **cucinino con frigoritero e blocco cottura** kitchenette with fridge and cooker

cuffia f: **cuffia da bagno** bathing cap

cugino(a) m/f cousin

cuocere: cuocere al forno to bake; **cuocere ai ferri** to grill

cuoio m leather

cuore m heart

curva f bend; corner; curve; **curva a gomito** hairpin bend; **curva senza visibilità** blind corner

cuscinetti mpl bearings (in car)

custode m caretaker

custodia valori f valuables accepted for safekeeping

C.V. horse power

da from; by; since; with

dama f draughts; partner (dancing)

danneggiare to spoil; to damage

dare to give; **dare su** to overlook; to give onto; **dare la precedenza (a destra)** give way (to traffic coming from the right)

data f date (day)

dati mpl data

dattero m date (fruit)

davanti in front; opposite

dazio m customs duty

decollo m takeoff

degustazione f: **degustazione caffè** specialist coffee shop and coffee bar; **degustazione vini** specialist wine bar

demi sec: spumante demi-sec m medium-dry sparkling wine

denominazione f: **denominazione di origine controllata** mark guaranteeing the quality and origin of a wine; **denominazione di origine controllata e garantita** as above, but of a higher standard: awarded to only a few top-quality wines

dentifricio m toothpaste

dentro in; inside

depositare to settle (wine); to deposit

deposito m deposit; **deposito bagagli** left luggage office; **deposito cauzionale** deposit; **deposito valori** place where valuables may be left

destinazione f destination; **con destinazione Messina** bound for Messina

destra f right

detersivo m soap powder; detergent

detrazione f deduction

dettatura f: **dettatura telegrammi** telemessage service

deviazione f diversion; detour

di of; some

dicembre m December

dichiarare to declare; **niente da**

dichiarare nothing to declare

dichiarazione f declaration; statement; **dichiarazione doganale** customs declaration

dieci ten

dietro behind; after

difficile difficult

diga f dam; dyke

digestivo m after-dinner liqueur

diluire to dilute

dindio m : **dindio ripieno** stuffed turkey

dintorni mpl surroundings

dio m god; **Dio** God

dipinto m painting

diramazione f fork

dire to tell; to say

diretto(a) direct; **treno diretto** through train

direttore m conductor (of orchestra); manager; president (of company); director (of firm)

direzione f management; direction; **direzione regionale del turismo** regional tourist board headquarters

diritto right; right side (of cloth etc); **diritto per esazioni in treno** fine payable if not in possession of a train ticket; **diritti portuali/ aeroportuali** harbour/airport taxes

diritto(a) straight; **sempre diritto** straight on

disco m disc; record; **disco orario** parking disc

discoteca f disco(thèque)

disdire to cancel

disegno m plan; design; pattern; drawing

dispiacere a to displease; **mi dispiace** (I'm) sorry

dispone(si) provided

disponibile available

dispositivo m gadget

disposizione f: **per disposizione di legge** by law; **siamo a vostra completa disposizione** we are entirely at your disposal

dissestato(a): strada dissestata road up

distanza f distance

distorsione f sprain

distributore m : **distributore automatico** vending machine; **distributore automatico di benzina** self-service petrol pump; **distributore di benzina** petrol pump

disturbare to disturb; **pregasi non disturbare** do not disturb

disturbo m trouble

ditta f business; firm; company

diurno(a) day(time); **programma diurno** daytime programme; **albergo diurno** public toilets with washing and shaving facilities etc

divano m sofa; divan; **divano letto** bed settee

diversi(e) several

diverso(a) different

divertente funny

divieto: è fatto severo divieto ... it is strictly forbidden to ...; **divieto di balneazione** no bathing; **divieto di parcheggio** no parking; **divieto di transito ai pedoni** pedestrians prohibited

divisa f : **divisa estera** foreign

currency

DOC *abbrev. of* **denominazione di origine controllata**

doccia *f* shower *(bath)*

DOCG *abbrev. of* **denominazione di origine controllata e garantita**

documenti *mpl* papers *(passport etc)*

dogana *f* customs

dolce[1] sweet; mild

dolce[2] *m* sweet; dessert, cake; **dolci assortiti** assorted cakes/desserts; **dolci della casa** our own cakes/desserts

dolcelatte *m* mild, creamy blue cheese

Dolcetto *m* dry red wine with slightly bitter taste

dolciumi *mpl* sweets

dolore *m* grief; pain

domanda *f* question; demand; application *(for job)*; **fare domanda per** to apply for

domani tomorrow

domattina tomorrow morning

domenica *f* Sunday

dondolare: non dondolare sit still

donna *f* woman; **donna delle pulizie** cleaning lady

dono *m* gift; donation

dopo after; afterward(s)

dopobarba *m* aftershave (lotion)

dopodomani the day after tomorrow

doppio(a) double

dove where; **di dove è?** where are you from?

dovere to have to; must

dragoncello *m* tarragon

drogheria *f* grocery shop

due two; **tutti(e) e due** both

duomo *m* cathedral

durante during

durare to last

duro(a) hard; tough; harsh

e and

è *see* GRAMMAR

E *abbrev. of* **est**

E road symbol for international route

ecc etc

eccedenza *f* excess; surplus

eccesso *m* excess; **eccesso di velocità** speeding

eccezionale exceptional

eccezione *f* exception

ecco here is/are

edicola *f* newsstand

edificio *m* building

effetto *m* effect; **effetti personali** belongings

efficace effective

egregio(a): Egregio Signor Smith Dear Mr Smith

elenco *m* list; **elenco telefonico** telephone directory

elettrauto *m* workshop for car electrical repairs; car electrician

elettricista *m* electrician

elettricità *f* electricity

elettrico(a) electric(al)

elettrodomestico *m* domestic (electrical) appliance

elettroricambi *mpl* electrical spares

elicottero *m* helicopter
emergenza *f* emergency
emicrania *f* migraine
enoteca *f* wine bar
ente *m* body; corporation; **ente nazionale/provinciale turismo** national/provincial tourist board
entrambi(e) both
entrare to come in; to enter; to go in
entrata *f* entrance; **entrata abbonati** season ticket holders' entrance; **entrata libera** free admission
epilessia *f* epilepsy
equino(a): carni equine *fpl* horsemeat
equipaggio *m* crew
equitazione *f* horse-riding
erba *f* grass
erbaceo(a): vino erbaceo wine with a flavour of herbs
erbe *fpl* herbs; **erbe aromatiche** herbs
erbette *fpl* beet tops
erboristeria *f* herbalist's (shop)
errore *m* error; mistake
eruzione *f* rash
esatto(a) exact; accurate
esaurito(a) exhausted; out of print; sold out; **tutto esaurito** sold out; house full
escluso(a): escluso taxi etc except for taxis etc; **escluse le bevande** excluding drinks
escursione *f* excursion; **escursioni in battello** boat trips
esente exempt; **esente da dogana/tasse** duty-/tax-free

esercizio *m* exercise; business; **questo esercizio resta chiuso nel giorno di ...** this shop (or restaurant etc) is closed on ...
esigenza *f* requirement
esperto(a) expert; experienced
esportare to export
esposto(a) exposed; **esposto(a) a nord** facing north
espresso *m* express letter; express train; espresso (coffee)
est *m* east
estate *f* summer
esterno(a) outside; external
estero(a) foreign; **all'estero** abroad
estetista *m/f* beautician
estintore *m* fire extinguisher
estivo(a) summer
estratto *m* : **estratto di carne** meat extract
età *f* age
etichetta *f* etiquette; tag; label
eventuale possible
evitare to avoid
extrasec: spumante extrasec *m* extra-dry sparkling wine

fabbrica *f* factory
fabbricare to manufacture; **fabbricato in serie** mass produced
facchino *m* porter *(for luggage)*
facile easy
facoltativo(a) optional
fagiano *m* pheasant
fagioli *mpl* beans; **fagioli borlotti** kidney beans; **fagioli con le cotiche** beans in a ham and tomato sauce with onion, garlic, basil, parsley

fagiolini *mpl* runner beans

falegname *m* carpenter; joiner

falò *m* bonfire

famiglia *m* family

familiare family; familiar

fanale *m* light *(on car)*; **fanali di posizione** sidelights; **fanali dei freni** stoplights

fango *m* mud

faraona *f* guinea fowl

farcito(a) stuffed *(chicken etc)*

fare to do; to make

farfalle *fpl* pasta bows

farina *f* flour; **farina di granturco** cornflour

farmacia *f* chemist's shop; **farmacie di turno** duty chemists

faro *m* headlight; lighthouse

fascia *f* band; bandage

fatelo da voi *m* do-it-yourself

fattoria *f* farm

fattorino d'albergo *m* bellboy

fattura *f* invoice; **la fattura si richiede all'atto del pagamento** an invoice should be requested when making payment

fave *fpl* broad beans

favore *m* : **per favore** please

fazzoletto di carta *m* tissue *(handkerchief)*

fazzoletto *m* (head) scarf

febbraio *m* February

febbre *f* fever; **febbre da fieno** hay fever

federa *f* pillowcase; pillowslip

fegatelli *mpl* : **fegatelli alla fiorentina** pig's liver kebabs with fried croutons, bay leaves, fennel, garlic

fegatini *mpl* : **fegatini d'anatra** duck livers; **fegatini di pollo** chicken livers

fegato *m* liver; **fegato di maiale/vitello** pig's/calf's liver; **fegato alla veneziana** calf's liver fried with onions

felicissimo(a) delighted

femminile feminine

fendinebbia: (proiettori) fendinebbia *mpl* fog lamps

feriale: giorno feriale working day; weekday

ferie *fpl* holiday(s)

ferita *f* wound; injury; cut

fermare to stop

fermarsi to stop

fermata *f* stop; **fermata dell'autobus** bus stop; **fermata a richiesta** request stop; **divieto di fermata** no waiting

fermo(a) stationary; off *(machine)*; **ferme restando le condizioni di cui sopra** in accordance with the terms as set out above

ferramenta *fpl* hardware

ferri *mpl* : **ai ferri** grilled

ferro *m* iron; **ferro da stiro** iron *(for clothes)*

ferrovia railway; **ferrovia pacchi dogana** border customs office for rail parcels

ferroviario(a) rail(way)

fesa *f*: **fesa di vitello** rump of veal

fessura *f* slot; crack

festa *f* party; holiday *(day)*; **festa danzante** dance

fetta *f* slice; **fette biscottate** rusks

fettuccine *fpl* ribbon-shaped pasta

FF SS Italian State Railways

fiammifero *m* match

fiasco *m* straw-covered flask

fico *m* fig

fiera *f* fair

fieristico(a): sede fieristica trade fair centre

figlia *f* daughter

figlio *m* son

fila *f* row; queue; **fare la fila** to queue

filetto *m* fillet; **filetto alla Carpaccio** raw strips of fillet steak with mayonnaise, cream, Worcester sauce, red peppers, capers and brandy; **filetto di manzo alla griglia** grilled fillet steak; **filetto al pepe verde** fillet steak with green peppercorns; **filetti di merluzzo/sogliola** cod/sole fillets

filiale *f* branch; subsidiary

filo di ferro *m* wire

filone *m* : **filone di vitello** veal marrow bone

filtro *m* filter; **con filtro** tipped (cigarettes)

finanziera *f* sauce made with truffles, mushrooms, offal and Marsala

fine *m* end; **fine settimana** weekend

finestra *f* window

finestrino *m* window (in car, train)

finire to finish

fino even; **fino a** until; as far as; **fino a 6** up to 6

finocchio *m* fennel; **semi di finocchio** fennel seeds

fiocco *m* flake

fioraio(a) *m/f* florist

fior di latte *m* cream ((ice-cream flavour))

fiore *f* flower; **fiori di zucca fritti** fried courgette flowers

fiorista *m/f* florist

Firenze *f* Florence

firma *f* signature

fiume *m* river

focaccia *f* kind of pizza; bun

folle mad; **in folle** in neutral (car)

fondale *m* bottom; **attenzione basso fondale** warning: shallow water

fondo *m* back (of room); bottom; **fondo stradale dissestato** uneven road surface

fonduta *f* melted cheese with milk, egg yolk and truffles

fontana *f* fountain

fonte *f* source

fontina *f* soft, creamy cheese from Piedmont

footing *m* jogging

foratura *f* puncture

forchetta *f* fork

forfora *f* dandruff

formaggio *m* cheese; **formaggi piccanti/teneri** strong/mild cheeses

fornaio *m* baker

fornello *m* stove; hotplate

fornitore *m* supplier

forno *m* oven

forse perhaps

forte strong; loud

forza *f* strength; force; **per causa di forza maggiore** by reason of an act of God; due to circumstances beyond one's control

foschia *f* mist

foto f photo

foto-ottica f photographic and optical instruments dealer

fototessera f passport(-type) photo

fra between; among(st); **fra 2 giorni** in 2 days

fragola f strawberry; **fragole al limone** strawberries with lemon juice and sugar; **fragole con la panna** strawberries and cream

frana f landslide

francese French

franchigia f: **in franchigia** duty free; **franchigia bagaglio** luggage allowance

Francia f France

francobollo m (postage) stamp

frappé m milk shake

Frascati m dry or medium-dry white wine from the Frascati area near Rome

fratello m brother

frattaglie fpl offal; giblets

frattura f fracture

frazione f village

freccette fpl darts

freddo(a) cold

freno m brake; **freno a mano** handbrake; **freno a pedale** footbrake

fresco(a) cool; fresh; wet (paint)

fricassea f: **coniglio/pollo etc in fricassea** rabbit/chicken etc fricassee

frigorifero m refrigerator

frittata f omelette; **frittata con le erbe/le verdure** omelette with herbs/vegetables

frittella f fritter

fritto m: **fritto misto** mixed fry

fritto(a) fried

frizione f clutch (of car)

frizzante fizzy; sparkling

fronte f forehead; **di fronte a** facing

frontiera f frontier; border

frullato m milkshake

frutta f fruit; **frutta secca** dried fruit

fruttato(a) fruity (wine)

fruttivendolo m greengrocer

frutto m fruit; **frutti di mare** seafood; **frutti di bosco** fruits of the forest (blackberries) etc

FS Italian State Railway

fuga f escape; leak (gas)

fumare to smoke

fumatore m smoker

fungo m mushroom; **funghi ovoli** royal agaric mushrooms; **funghi porcini** boletus mushrooms; **funghi secchi** dried mushrooms

funzionare to work (mechanism)

fuoco m fire; focus; **fuochi d'artificio** fireworks

fuori outside; out (not at home)

fusibile m fuse

gabinetto m toilet; **gabinetto medico** doctor's surgery

galleria f tunnel; gallery; circle (in theatre); arcade; **prima galleria** dress circle; **galleria interi/ridotti** full-price/concessionary circle tickets; **galleria d'arte** art gallery

gamba f leg

gamberetto m shrimp; prawn

gambero m crayfish

garanzia f guarantee; warranty;

garanzia assicurativa insurance cover; **garanzie infortuni al conducente** cover in the event of an accident to the driver

gasolio *m* diesel oil

gassato(a): bevanda gassata fizzy drink

gassosa fizzy

gelateria *f* ice-cream shop

gelatina *f* jelly

gelato *m* ice-cream

gelo *m* frost

genere *m* kind *(type)*; gender

generi alimentari *mpl.* foodstuffs

genitori *mpl* parents

gennaio *m* January

Genova *f* Genoa

Germania *f* Germany

gesso *m* chalk; plaster *(for limb)*

gettare to throw; **non gettare alcun oggetto dal finestrino** do not throw anything out of the window

gettone *m* token *(for machine, telephone)*; chip *(in gambling)*; counter

gettoniera *f* telephone-token dispenser

ghiaccio *m* ice

ghiacciolo *m* ice lolly

ghiaia *f* gravel

giacca *f* jacket; **giacca di salvataggio** life jacket

giallo(a) yellow

giardinetta *f* estate *(car)*

giardino *m* garden

ginepro *m* juniper; **bacche di ginepro** juniper berries

Ginevra *f* Geneva

gingerino *m* drink similar to ginger ale

ginocchio *m* knee

giocare to play; to gamble

giocattolo *m* toy

gioco *m* game; **gioco d'azzardo** gambling

gioielli *mpl* jewellery

gioielliere *m* jeweller

giornalaio *m* newsagent

giornale *m* newspaper

giornalista *m/f* journalist

giornata *f* day *(length)*

giorno *m* day; **giorno festivo** holiday; **giorno feriale** weekday; **giorno di mercato** market-day

giovane young; young person

giovedì *m* Thursday

girare to turn; to spin

giro *m* tour; turn; **fare un giro in macchina** to go for a drive

gita *f* trip; excursion

giù down; downstairs

giugno *m* June

gli the; to him/it

globale inclusive *(costs)*

gnocchi *mpl* small dumplings made of potato or semolina; **gnocchi di semolino alla romana** semolina dumplings made with butter, egg yolks, milk and nutmeg

goccia *f* drop *(of liquid)*; drip

gola *f* throat; gorge

golfo *m* gulf

gomma *f* rubber; tyre

gommone *m* dinghy *(inflatable)*

gonfiare to inflate

gonfio(a) swollen

gonna f skirt

gorgonzola m rich, soft blue-veined cheese with a pungent smell

gradazione f: **a bassa gradazione alcolica** low in alcohol

gradevole pleasant

gradinata f flight of steps; terracing

gradino m step; stair

gradire to accept; to like; **gradisce qualcosa da bere?** would you like something to drink?

grado m grade; standard; degree

grana m hard cheese similar to Parmesan

Gran Bretagna f Great Britain

grancevola f spiny spider crab

granchio m crab; **polpa di granchio** crab meat

grande great; large; big

grandine f hail

granita f water ice

grano m grain

granturco m maize

grappa f spirit distilled from remains of grapes after pressing

gratinato(a) sprinkled with grated cheese and breadcrumbs and browned in the oven

grattacielo m skyscraper

gratuito(a) free; **il servizio è gratuito** the service is free of charge

grazie thank you

grazioso(a) charming; graceful

Grecia f Greece

greco(a) Greek

grigio(a) grey

griglia f grill; **alla griglia** grilled

grigliata f grill; **grigliata mista** mixed grill

Grignolino m dry red wine from Piedmont, with the scent of roses

grissino m bread-stick

grongo m conger eel

grossista m/f wholesaler

grosso(a) big; thick

groviera f mild cheese with holes: Italian version of the Swiss cheese, gruyère

gruppo m group; **gruppo sanguigno** blood group

gruviera f see **groviera**

guado m ford

guanto m glove

guardare to watch; to look (at)

guardaroba m wardrobe; cloakroom

guardia f guard; **Guardia di Finanza** Customs and Excise

guardiano m warder; caretaker

guasto m failure (mechanical)

guasto(a) out of order

guerra f war

guida f directory; guide; guidebook; **guida a sinistra** left-hand drive; **guida telefonica** telephone directory

guidare to drive; to steer

guidatore m driver

guinzaglio m: **cani al guinzaglio** dogs must be on a lead

guscio m shell

gustare to taste; to enjoy

gusto m taste; flavour

i the

ieri yesterday; **ieri l'altro** the day before yesterday

il the

illimitato(a) unlimited

imbarcarsi to embark

imbarcazione f boat

imbarco m boarding; **carta d'imbarco** boarding card

imbottigliato(a) bottled

immergere to dip (into liquid)

immersione f: **immersione in apnea** diving without breathing apparatus

immondizie fpl rubbish

impanato coated with breadcrumbs

imparare to learn

impasto m mixture

imperatore m emperor

impermeabile m waterproof; raincoat

impero m empire

impiegato(a) m/f employee

importare to import; to matter; **non importa** it doesn't matter

importo m (total) amount

imposta f tax (on income); shutter (on window); **imposta sul valore aggiunto** value-added tax

in in; to; into

inadempienza f: **eventuali inadempienze dei nostri agenti di viaggio ...** any negligence on the part of our travel agents ...

incantevole charming

incaricarsi di to take charge of

incendio m fire

incidente m accident; **incidente stradale/aereo** road accident/plane crash

incluso(a) included; enclosed; inclusive

incontrare to meet

incrocio m crossroads; **incrocio a T** T-junction

indicazioni fpl directions

indice m index; contents

indietro m backwards; back; behind

indirizzo m address

indivia f endive

indomani m : **l'indomani** the next day

indovinare to guess

indumento m garment

infatti in fact; actually

infermeria f infirmary

infezione f infection

infiammabile inflammable

infiammazione f inflammation

influenza f influence; flu

informare to inform; **informarsi (di)** to inquire (about)

informazioni fpl information; **per informazioni e prenotazioni di gruppi ...** for information and group bookings ...

infrangibile unbreakable

ingegnere m engineer

Inghilterra f England

inglese English

ingombrante: bagaglio ingombrante luggage exceeding the dimensions allowed

ingombrare: non ingombrare l'uscita

do not obstruct the exit

ingorgo m blockage; **ingorgo stradale** traffic jam

ingresso m entry; entrance; **prezzo d'ingresso** admission fee; **ingresso libero** admission free; no obligation to buy; **ingresso a pagamento** admission charge; **ingresso pedonale** pedestrian entrance; **ingresso riservato al personale** staff only; **ingresso vietato ai non addetti ai lavori** no entry to unauthorised personnel

ingrosso: all'ingrosso wholesale

iniezione f injection

inizio m start

innocuo(a) harmless

inoltre besides

insaccati mpl sausages

insalata f salad; **insalata verde** green salad; **insalata mista/di pomodori/di riso/di cetrioli** mixed/tomato/rice/cucumber salad; **insalata di pesce** seafood salad; **insalata russa** mixed boiled vegetables in mayonnaise

insegnante m/f teacher

inserire to insert; **inserire le banconote una per volta** insert the banknotes one at a time

insettifugo m insect repellent

insetto m insect

insieme together; outfit

insolazione f sunstroke

insulina f insulin

interno m inside; telephone extension; flat number

interno(a) internal

intero(a) whole

interpretazione f interpretation

interruttore m switch

interurbano(a) long-distance

intervallo m half-time; interval (in performance)

intervento m operation (medical)

intestato(a) a registered in the name of; made out in the name of

intimi donna mpl ladies' underwear

intingolo m sauce; tasty dish

intorno round

intossicazione alimentare f food poisoning

introdurre to introduce

inutile unnecessary; useless

invalido(a) disabled; invalid

invano in vain

invece instead; but; **invece di** instead of

inverno m winter

inversione f U turn

invitare to invite

invito m invitation

involtino m stuffed meat roll

iodio m iodine

ippodromo m racecourse

Irlanda f Ireland

irlandese Irish

iscritto m member; **per iscritto** in writing

iscrizione f inscription; enrolment; registration

isola f island; **isola pedonale** pedestrian precinct

isolato m block

istituto m institute; **istituto di**

bellezza beauty salon

istruttore(trice) *m/f*
instructor/instructress

istruzioni *fpl* instructions;
directions

Italia *f* Italy

itinerario *m* route; **itinerario di
massima** general itinerary; **itinerari
d'arte** routes of artistic interest;
itinerario turistico scenic route

I.V.A. *f* V.A.T.

jolly *m* joker *(cards)*

l' the; him; her; it; you

la the; her; it; you

là there; **per di là** that way

labbro *m* lip

lacca *f* lacquer; hair spray

Lacrima Christi *m* dry red/white
wine produced in Campania

laggiù down there; over there

lago *m* lake

Lambrusco *m* sparkling red wine
from Emilia-Romagna

lampone *m* raspberry

lana *f* wool

lanciare to throw; to launch

largo(a) wide; broad; **al largo**
offshore

lasagne *fpl* thin layers of pasta with
meat sauce, white sauce, and
grated cheese, baked in the oven;
lasagne verdi thin layers of spinach
pasta, served as above

lasciare to leave; to let go of; to let
(allow); **lasciare libero il passaggio**
keep clear

lassativo *m* laxative

lassù up there

laterale: **via laterale** *f* side street

latte *m* milk; **latte condensato**
condensed milk; **latte detergente**
cleansing milk; **latte intero** full-
cream milk; **latte macchiato** hot
milk with a dash of coffee; **latte in
polvere** dried milk; **latte scremato**
skimmed milk

latteria *f* dairy

lattuga *f* lettuce; **lattuga romana** cos
lettuce

lavabile washable

lavaggio *m* washing; **qui lavaggio
rapido** rapid car wash; **per lavaggi
frequenti** for frequent shampooing

lavanderia *f* laundry *(place)*;
servizio lavanderia e stireria
laundry and ironing service

lavare to wash; **lavare a secco** to
dry-clean

lavasecco *m* dry-cleaner's *(shop)*

lavatrice *f* washing machine

lavoro *m* work; **lavori stradali** road
works; **lavori in corso** work in
progress; road works ahead

le the; them; to her/it; to you

legenda *f* key

legge *f* law

leggere to read; **leggere
attentamente le avvertenze** read the
instructions carefully

leggero(a) light *(not heavy)*; weak;
mild; minor

legumi *mpl* : **legumi secchi** dried
pulses

lei she; her; you; **Lei** you

lente *f* lens *(of glasses)*; **lenti a**

contatto contact lenses

lenticchie *fpl* lentils

lenzuolo *m* sheet

lepre *f* hare; **lepre in salmì** jugged hare

lesso *m* boiled meat

lettino *m* cot

letto *m* bed; **letto a una piazza** single bed; **letto matrimoniale** double bed; **letti a castello** bunk beds; **letti gemelli** twin beds

levata *f* collection (of mail); **orario della levata** collection times

lezione *f* lesson; lecture

lì there

libero(a) free; clear (not blocked); vacant (seat, toilet)

libreria *f* bookshop

libretto *m* booklet; **libretto di circolazione** logbook (of car); **libretto degli assegni** cheque-book

libro *m* book

lieto(a) glad

molto lieto pleased to meet you

limite *m* limit; boundary; **limite di velocità** speed limit

limonata *f* lemonade

limone *m* lemon

linea *f* line; **linea urbana** urban bus service; **linee marittime** sea routes; shipping lines; **Linee FS** Italian State railway network

lingua *f* language; tongue; **lingua salmistrata** pickled ox tongue

lino *m* linen

liofilizzato(a) freeze-dried

liquidazione *f* liquidation sale

liquirizia *f* licorice

liquore *m* liqueur

liquori *mpl* spirits

liquoroso(a): vino liquoroso dessert wine

liscio(a) smooth; straight

lista *f* list; **lista dei vini** wine list; **lista d'attesa** waiting list; **lista delle pietanze** menu

listino prezzi *m* price list

litro *m* litre

livello *m* level; **livello del mare** sea level

lo the; him; it

locale *m* room; place; **locale notturno** nightclub

località *f*: **località balneare/di villeggiatura** seaside/holiday resort

locanda *f* inn

locomotiva *f* engine (of train)

loggione *m*: **il loggione** the gods (in theatre)

Londra *f* London

lontano far

lordo(a) gross; pre-tax

loro they; them; to them; you; to you; **Loro** you; to you

lotto *m* lottery; lot (at auction)

lozione *f* lotion

luccio *m* pike

luce *f* light

luglio *m* July

lumache *fpl* snails

luna *f* moon; **luna di miele** honeymoon

luna-park *m* amusement park

lunedì *m* Monday

lungo(a) long; **lungo la strada** along

the street; **a lungo** for a long time
lungomare m promenade; seafront
luogo m place
lusso m luxury

ma but
maccheroni mpl macaroni;
maccheroni alla siciliana macaroni
in a sauce containing tomato,
capers, garlic, green and black
olives, chilli pepper; **maccheroni
alla chitarra** macaroni in a sauce
containing bacon, tomato, cheese,
onion, basil
macchina f car; machine; **macchina
fotografica** camera; **macchina
sportiva** sports car
macedonia f fruit salad
macelleria f butcher's (shop)
macinato(a) ground (coffee)
madera m Madeira (wine)
madre f mother
magazzino m store room;
warehouse; **grande magazzino**
department store
maggio m May
maggiorazione f increase
maggiore larger; greater; largest;
greatest
maglieria f knitwear
magro(a) thin (person); lean (meat)
mai never; ever
maiale m pig; pork; **maiale al latte**
pork cooked in milk with bacon,
garlic, cinnamon and rosemary;
maiale arrosto roast pork
maialino m : **maialini da latte**
suckling pigs

maionese f mayonnaise
mais m maize
mal m
male¹ badly (not well)
male² m pain; ache; **mal d'auto** car-
sickness; **mal di mare** seasickness;
mal di cuore/di fegato heart/liver
complaint; **mal di denti/di gola/
d'orecchi/di stomaco/di testa**
toothache/sore throat/earache/
stomach ache/headache
malgrado in spite of
maltempo m bad weather
Malvasia f sweet, aromatic dessert
wine
mamma f mum(my)
mancato(a): mancate coincidenze
fpl missed (rail/air etc)
connections
mancia f tip (money given)
mandarino m mandarin (orange)
mandorla f almond
maneggio m riding school
mangia-e-bevi m ice-cream with
nuts, fruit and liqueur
mangiare to eat
Manica f Channel
maniglia f handle; strap (on bus)
mano f hand; trick (in cards);
fatto(a) a mano handmade
manovella f handle (for winding)
mantenere: mantenere la destra
keep right
Mantova f Mantua
manzo m beef
marcia f march; gear (of car)
marciapiede m pavement;
platform

mare *m* sea; seaside

marea *f* tide; **c'è alta/bassa marea** the tide is in/out

marina *f* navy

marito *m* husband

maritozzo *m* sort of currant bun

marmellata *f* jam; **marmellata d'arance** marmalade

marmitta *f* silencer (on car)

marmo *m* marble (material)

marrone brown; chestnut

Marsala *m* dessert wine from Sicily

martedì *m* Tuesday; **martedì grasso** Shrove Tuesday

marzo *m* March

mascarpone *m* soft, creamy cheese often served as a dessert

maschile masculine

massimale *m* maximum sum insurable

massimo(a) maximum

masticare to chew

materassino *m* air bed

matrice *f* stub (counterfoil)

mattina *f* morning

mattino *m* morning

mattone *m* brick

medaglioni *mpl* : **medaglioni di filetto/di pollo** round fillets of beef/chicken

medicina *f* medicine; **medicina d'urgenza** emergency treatment

medico *m* doctor

medusa *f* jellyfish

meglio better; best

mela *f* apple; **mela cotogna** quince

melagrana *f* pomegranate

melanzana *f* aubergine; **melanzane alla parmigiana** aubergines baked with tomatoes, Parmesan cheese and spices; **melanzane ripiene** stuffed aubergines

melassa *f* treacle

melone *m* melon; **melone ghiacciato** iced melon

membro *m* member

meno less; minus

mensa *f* canteen

mensile monthly

menta *f* mint (herb)

mentre while; whereas

menù *m* : **menù del giorno** menu of the day; **menù turistico** tourist or low-price menu

mercatino *m* : **mercatino dell'usato** flea market

mercato *m* market; **Mercato Comune** Common Market; **mercato del pesce** fish market

merce *f* : **la merce si paga alle casse del piano dove è stata scelta** goods must be paid for on the floor from which they have been selected

merceria *f* haberdashery

merci *fpl* freight; goods

mercoledì *m* Wednesday

merenda *f* snack

meridionale southern

merlango *m* whiting

Merlot *m* dry red table wine

merluzzo *m* cod

mese *m* month

messa *f* mass (church); **messa in piega** set (of hair)

metà *f* half

metropolitana f underground

mettere to put; to put on (clothes); **mettere in comunicazione** to put through (on phone)

mezzanotte f midnight

mezzo m means; means of transport; middle

mezzo(a) half

mezzogiorno m midday; noon; **il Mezzogiorno** the south of Italy

mezz'ora f half-an-hour

mi me; to me; myself

miele m honey

migliore better; best

mille thousand

minestra f soup; **minestra in brodo** clear soup with rice or noodles; **minestra di verdura** vegetable soup

minestrone m thick vegetable soup; **minestrone alla genovese** vegetable soup flavoured with cheese and herb mixture (pesto)

minore: vietato ai minori di anni 18 no admission to anyone under 18 years of age

minorenne under age

mirtillo m cranberry

miscela f blend

misto m : **misto mare** mixed fish salad

misto(a) mixed

misura f measure; measurement; **fatto(a) su misura** made-to-measure

mitili mpl mussels

mittente m/f sender

MM abbrev. of **metropolitana**

mobili mpl furniture

moda f fashion

modalità f: **secondo le modalità previste** according to what has already been agreed; **modalità di pagamento** method of payment; **seguire le modalità d'uso** follow the instructions

modo m way; manner

modulo m form (document)

moglie f wife

mollica f: **mollica (di pane)** crumb

molluschi mpl molluscs

molo m pier; **molo per attracco** docking pier

molti(e) many

molto a lot; much; very

molto(a) much; **molta gente** lots of people

monastero m monastery

moneta f coin

montagna f mountain

Montepulciano m dry or sweet red wine from Tuscany; a type of red-wine grape

montone m : **carne di montone** mutton; **giacca di montone** sheepskin jacket

moquette f wall-to-wall carpet(ing)

mora f blackberry

mortadella f type of salted pork meat

morto(a) dead

mosca f fly

moscato m muscatel: red or white dessert wine; **moscato spumatizzato** sparkling muscatel; **Moscato d'Asti** sweet, sparkling white wine

moscerino m gnat

moscone m pedalo (with oars)

mosella *m* Moselle *(wine)*

mostarda *f* mustard

mostra *f* show; exhibition; **mostra convegno** conference and exhibition

mostrare to show

motocicletta *f* motorbike

motore *m* engine; motor; **vietato tenere motori e luci non elettriche accese** switch off engine and extinguish any cigarettes

motoscafo *m* motorboat

mozzarella *f* moist Neapolitan curd cheese; **mozzarella in carrozza** mozzarella with either anchovies or ham between two slices of bread, fried in batter

mulino *m* mill

multa *f* fine

municipio *m* town hall

muratura *f*: **villette in muratura** stonebuilt or brickbuilt villas

muro *m* wall

museo *m* museum; **museo civico di storia naturale** municipal museum of natural history

musica *f* music; **musica leggera/da camera** light/chamber music

nafta *f* diesel oil

Napoli *f* Naples

nascita *f* birth

nasello *m* hake

Natale *m* Christmas

nato(a) born

navata *f* nave

nave *f* ship

nave-traghetto *f* ferry

nazione *f* nation

né ... né neither ... nor

neanche not even; neither

nebbia *f* fog

Nebbiolo *m* light, dry red wine from Piedmont

negozio *m* shop

nemmeno/neppure not even; neither

nero(a) black

nervetti *mpl*: **nervetti in insalata** thin strips of sinewy beef or veal served cold with beans, shallots and pickles

nessuno(a) no; any; nobody; none; anybody

netto(a) net; **al netto di IVA** net of VAT

neve *f* snow

nevicare to snow

nevischio *m* sleet

niente nothing; anything

Nizza *f* Nice

noce *f* walnut

nocivo(a) harmful

nodo *m* knot; bow *(ribbon)*; **nodo ferroviario** junction *(railway)*

noleggio *m*: **noleggio biciclette** bicycles for hire; **noleggio furgoni** vans for hire

nolo *m* = **noleggio**

nome *m* name; first name

non not

non-fumatore *m* non-smoker *(person)*

nonna *f* grandmother

nonno *m* grandfather

nord *m* north

notiziario m news (on TV etc)

nove nine

novembre m November

nubile single (woman)

nulla nothing; anything

nullo(a) void (contract)

numero m number (figure); act (at circus etc); issue (of magazine); size (of shoes)

nuotare to swim

nuovo(a) new; **di nuovo** again

nuvoloso(a) cloudy

obbligo m obligation

obliterare to stamp (ticket); **lato da obliterare** side to be stamped

obliteratrice f stamping machine

oca f goose

occasione f opportunity; occasion; bargain

occhiali mpl glasses; goggles; **occhiali da sole** sunglasses

occuparsi: me ne occupo io I'll take care of it

occupato(a) busy; engaged

odierno(a): in data odierna today

offerta f: **in offerta (speciale)** on (special) offer

officina f workshop; **officina autorizzata** authorised garage; **officina per autovetture nazionali ed estere** repairs carried out on all makes of car

oggettistica f fancy goods

oggi today

ogni every; each

Olanda f Holland

oleodotto m pipeline

olio m oil; **olio solare** suntan oil; **olio d'oliva** olive oil

oltre beyond; besides

ombrellone m sunshade (over table); beach umbrella

omogeneizzati mpl baby foods

onda f wave

opuscolo m brochure

ora¹ now

ora² f hour; **che ora è?** what's the time?

orario m timetable; schedule; **in orario** punctual; on schedule; **orario di apertura/chiusura** opening/closing times; **orario di cassa** banking hours; **orario delle partenze** timetable for departures; **orario degli uffici per il pubblico** hours of opening to the public; **orario di vendita** opening hours; **orario per visitatori** visiting times

orata f sea bream

ordinare to order (goods, meal)

ordinazione f order (for goods)

oreficeria f jeweller's (shop)

ormeggiare to moor

oro m gold; **placcato oro** gold-plated

orologeria m watchmaker's (shop)

ortaggi mpl vegetables

ortofrutticolo(a): mercato ortofrutticolo fruit and vegetable market

Orvieto m light, straw-coloured wine from Umbria: dry, sweet or semi-sweet

orzo m barley; **orzo tostato solubile** instant barley coffee

ospedale m hospital

ospite *m/f* guest; host; hostess

osso *m* bone

ossobuco *m* marrowbone; stew made with knuckle of veal in tomato and wine

ostello *m* : **ostello della gioventù** *m* youth hostel

osteria *f* inn

ostrica *f* oyster

ottenere to obtain; to get; **ottenere la linea** to get through *(on phone)*

ottico *m* optician

otto eight

ottobre *m* October

ovest *m* west

ovino(a): carni ovine *fpl* lamb and mutton

pacco *m* parcel

padella *f* frying pan

Padova *f* Padua

padre *m* father

padrone(a) *m/f* landlord/landlady

paesaggio *m* scenery; countryside

paese *m* country; land

paesino *m* village

pagamento *m* payment; **pagamento alla consegna** cash on delivery; **pagamento anticipato** payment in advance

pagare to pay; to pay for

paglia *f* : **paglia e fieno** white and green pasta ribbons

pagnotta *f* round loaf

palasport *m* sports stadium

palazzo *m* building; palace; **palazzo communale** town hall; **palazzo dei congressi** conference

centre; **palazzo dello sport** sports stadium

palco *m* platform

palcoscenico *m* stage

palestra *f* gym(nasium)

palla *f* ball

pallone *m* balloon; football

palma *f* palm tree

pan *m* = **pane**

pancetta *f* bacon

pandoro *m* type of sponge cake eaten at Christmas

pane *m* bread; loaf (of bread); **pane carrè** sandwich bread; **pane e coperto** cover charge; **pane integrale** wholemeal bread; **pan di Spagna** sponge; **pane di segale** rye bread

panetteria *f* bakery

panettone *m* very light cake containing sultanas and crystallized fruit, traditionally eaten at Christmas

panforte *m* nougat-type delicacy from Siena

pangrattato *m* breadcrumbs

panificio *m* bakery

panino *m* roll; **panino imbottito** sandwich; **panini caldi** hot rolls

panna *f* cream; **panna montata** whipped cream

pannocchia *f* corn-on-the-cob

pannolino *m* nappy

panzarotto *m* fried savoury turnover with a filling of mozzarella, bacon, egg and sometimes tomatoes and anchovies

papà *m* dad(dy)

pappardelle *fpl* wide strips of pasta

parcheggio *m* car-park; **parcheggio custodito/incustodito** attended/ unattended car-park

parchimetro *m* parking meter

parco *m* park; **parco demaniale** public park; **parco giochi bambini** children's play park; **parco marino** nature reserve for marine life

parente *m/f* relation; relative

Parigi *f* Paris

parmigiano *m* Parmesan: hard, tangy cheese often used in cooking

parrucchiere(a) *m/f* hairdresser

parte *f* share; part; side

partenza *f* departure

partire to go; to leave

partita *f* match; game

Pasqua *f* Easter

passaggio *m* passage; gangway; **dare un passaggio a** to give a lift to; **passaggio a livello** level crossing; **passaggio pedonale** pedestrian crossing

passaporto *m* passport; **passaporto collettivo** group passport

passato *m* past; **passato freddo di pomodoro** chilled tomato soup; **passato di patate/piselli** creamed potatoes/peas; **passato di verdura** cream of vegetable soup

passeggero(a) *m/f* passenger

passeggiata *f* walk; stroll; **passeggiata lungomare** promenade

passera *f* plaice

passito *m* sweet wine made with raisins

passo *m* pace; step; pass *(in*

mountains); **passo carrabile** keep clear

pasta *f* pastry; pasta; dough; **pasta di acciughe** anchovy paste; **pasta e ceci/fagioli** chick pea/bean and pasta soup; **pasta frolla** shortcrust pastry; **pasta di mandorle** almond paste; **pasta sfoglia** puff pastry; **pasta all'uovo** egg pasta

pastasciutta *f* pasta served in a sauce, not in soup

pasticceria *f* cake shop

pasticcino *m* petit four

pasticcio *m* muddle; pie *(meat)*; **pasticcio di lasagne** wide strips of pasta in layers, with meat sauce, white sauce and cheese

pasto *m* meal

pastorizzato pasteurised

pastoso(a): vino pastoso mellow wine

patata *f* potato; **patate arrosto/al forno** roast/baked potatoes; **patate fritte** chips; **patate lesse/novelle/in padella/saltate** boiled/new/fried/ sautéed potatoes

patatine *fpl* crisps

patente *f* licence; driving licence

pattinaggio *m* skating

pavimento *m* floor

pecorino *m* hard, tangy sheep's-milk cheese

pedaggio *m* toll

pedicure *m* chiropodist

pedone *m* pedestrian

pelati *mpl* : **(pomodori) pelati** peeled tomatoes

pelle *f* skin; hide; leather; **pelle scamosciata** suede

pelletterie *fpl* leather goods

pellicceria *f* furrier's (shop); furs

pellicola *f* film *(for camera)*

penale *f* penalty clause

pendenza *f* slope

pendio *m* hill; slope

penne *fpl* quill-shaped tubes of pasta; **penne all'arrabbiata** penne in a spicy sauce of tomatoes, mushrooms, bacon, chilli pepper, basil and garlic; **penne ai funghi** penne with mushrooms, parsley, cream, whisky and butter

pensione *f* boarding house; pension; **pensione completa** full board; **mezza pensione** half board

Pentecoste *f* Whitsun; Whitsunday

peoci *mpl* mussels

pepato(a) peppery

pepe *m* pepper

peperonata *f* stew of peppers, aubergines, tomatoes, onion, garlic, oregano and basil

peperoncino *m* chilli pepper

peperone *m* pepper *(capsicum)*; **peperone verde/rosso** green/red pepper; **peperoni ripieni** stuffed peppers

per for; per; in order to

pera *f* pear

percentuale *f* percentage

perché why; because; in order that

percorrenza *f*: **biglietto con percorrenza superiore/inferiore a 100 chilometri** ticket for journeys of more than/less than 100 kilometres

percorribilità *f*: **percorribilità strade** traffic information service

percorso *m* journey; route; **percorso panoramico** scenic route

pericolante unsafe

pericolo *m* danger

pericoloso(a) dangerous

periferia *f* outskirts; suburbs

permanente *f* perm; **permanente continua** parking restrictions still apply

permanenza *f*: **buona permanenza!** enjoy your stay!

permesso *m* permission; permit; **permesso!** excuse me *(to get past someone)*; **permesso di soggiorno** residence permit

pernice *f* partridge

pernottamento *m* overnight stay

perquisizione *f*: **sono previste perquisizioni personali** searches will be carried out

personale *m* staff; **personale di sicurezza** security staff

p. es. e.g.

pesca *f* angling; fishing; peach; **pesche al vino rosso** peaches in red wine with cinnamon and sugar

pescatore *m* angler; fisherman

pesce *m* fish; **pesce persico** perch; **pesce spada** swordfish

pescheria *f* fishmonger's shop

pescivendolo *m* fishmonger's (shop)

pesto *m*: **pesto alla genovese** sauce made with fresh basil, pine kernels, garlic and cheese

petto *m* breast; chest

pezzo *m* piece; cut *(of meat)*; **pezzo di ricambio** spare *(part)*

piacere¹ to please; **le/ti/vi piace?** do

you like it?

piacere² *m* enjoyment; pleasure; **piacere di conoscerla** pleased to meet you

piano¹ slowly; quietly

piano² *m* floor *(storey)*; plan; **piani inferiori/superiori** on the lower/upper floors

pianobar *m* bar offering musical entertainment

pianoterra *m* ground floor

pianta *f* map *(of town)*; plan

pianterreno *m* ground floor

pianura *f* plain

piastra *f*: **panini alla piastra** toasted sandwiches; **formaggio alla piastra** grilled cheese

piatti *mpl*: **piatti pronti/da farsi** prepared dishes/dishes requiring preparation

piatto *m* dish; course; plate; **primo piatto** entrée

piazza *f* square

piazzale *m* open square; service area

piazzola *f*: **piazzola (di sosta)** lay-by

piccante spicy; hot

picco *m*: **a picco sul mare** rising straight from the sea

piccolo(a) little; small

piede *m* foot; **a piedi** on foot

pieno(a) full

pietra *f* stone

pillola *f* pill

pineta *f* pinewood

pino *m* pine

pinoli *mpl* pine kernels

Pinot *m*: **Pinot bianco** dry, aromatic

white wine from north-east Italy; **Pinot grigio** dry, aromatic and full-bodied white wine from the same area as 'Pinot bianco'; **Pinot nero** dry red wine with a fruity flavour, from the same area as the white Pinot

pioggia *f* rain

piovere to rain; **piove** it's raining

piroscafo *m* steamer

piscina *f* swimming pool; **piscina comunale** public swimming pool

piselli *mpl* peas

pista *f* track; race track; **pista da ballo** dance floor; **pista per principianti** nursery slope; **pista da sci** ski run

più more; most; plus

pizza *f*: **pizza alla diavola** pizza with spicy salami; **pizza margherita** pizza with tomato, mozzarella and oregano; **pizza napoletana** pizza with tomato, garlic and oregano; **pizza ai quattro formaggi** pizza with four kinds of cheese melted on top

pizzaiola *f*: **alla pizzaiola** with tomato, garlic and oregano sauce

pizzico *m* pinch; sting

placcato(a): **placcato oro/argento** gold-/silver-plated

platea *f* stalls; **platea interi/ridotti** full-price/concessionary seats in the stalls

pneumatico *m* tyre

po' *see* **poco(a)**

pochi(e) few

poco(a) little; not much; **un po'** a little

poi then

polenta f sort of thick porridge made with maize flour; **polenta e osei** small birds, spit-roasted and served with polenta

polizia f police; **polizia ferroviaria** railway police; **polizia stradale** traffic police

pollame m poultry

pollo m chicken; **pollo alla diavola** grilled chicken, highly spiced; **pollo allo spiedo** spit-roasted chicken

polpette fpl meatballs

polpettone m meat loaf

polpo m octopus

poltrona f seat in the stalls (theatre)

pomeriggio m afternoon

pomodoro m tomato

pompa f pump

pompelmo m grapefruit

pompieri mpl firemen

ponce m punch (drink)

ponte m bridge; deck; **ponte a pedaggio** toll bridge

pontile m jetty

porchetta f roast suckling pig

porro m leek

porta f door; gate; goal; **porta antipanico/di sicurezza** emergency exit

portare to carry; to bring; to wear

portata f course; range; capacity

portatore m : **pagabile al portatore** payable to the bearer

porticciolo m marina

portico m porch

portiere m porter (doorkeeper); janitor

portineria f caretaker's lodge

porto m port; harbour; **porto di scalo** port of call

porzione f portion; helping

posologia f dosage

posta f mail; stake; odds; **per posta aerea** by air mail; **posta raccomandata** registered mail; **fermo posta** poste restante

Poste fpl Post Office

posteggio m car park; **posteggio per tassì** taxi rank

posto m place; position; job; seat; **posto di blocco** road block; border post; **posto riservato ad invalidi di guerra e del lavoro** seat reserved for disabled persons; **posto di soccorso** first-aid centre; **posto telefonico pubblico** public telephone; **posti in piedi** standing room; **posti a sedere** seating capacity; **posti prenotati** reserved seats

potabile drinking; drinkable

pranzo m lunch

preavviso m advance notice; **comunicazioni con preavviso** person-to-person calls

precotto(a) ready-cooked

predeterminare: **predeterminare l'importo desiderato** select the amount required

prefisso m prefix; **prefisso (teleselettivo)** dialling code

pregare to pray; **si prega ...** please...

prego don't mention it!; after you!

prelievo m withdrawal; collection; blood sample; **prelievo gettoni e monete respinti** returned tokens and coins

preludio *m* overture

pré-maman *m* maternity dress

premere to push; to press

prendere to take; to get; to catch

prenotare to book; to reserve

prenotazione *f* reservation; **prenotazione obbligatoria** seats must be booked

presentare to introduce

presentarsi to report; to check in *(at airport)*

preservativo *m* condom

prestazioni *fpl* services; **prestazioni ambulatoriali** outpatients' department

prestigiatore *m* conjuror

prevendita *f*: **biglietti in prevendita** tickets may be purchased in advance

previo(a): **previa autorizzazione delle autorità competenti** upon authorization from the relevant authorities

previsione *f* forecast; **previsioni del tempo** weather forecast

previsto(a): **all'ora prevista** at the scheduled time; **come previsto** as expected

prezzemolo *m* parsley

prezzo *m* price; **prezzo fisso** set price; **prezzo di catalogo** list price; **prezzo al minuto** retail price; **prezzo d'ingresso** entrance fee

prima[1] before; first; earlier

prima[2] *f* première

primo(a) first; top; early; **solo prima classe senza prenotazione** only first-class passengers may travel

without a reserved seat

principiante *m/f* beginner

privo(a) di lacking in

prodotto *m* product; commodity

produzione *f* production; output; **gelati di produzione propria** our own ice cream

profondità *f* depth

profumeria *f* perfumery; perfume shop

programma *m* programme; syllabus; schedule; **fuori programma** supporting programme *(at cinema)*

proibire to ban; to prohibit

proiezione *f*: **proiezioni cinematografiche** film shows

pronto(a) ready; **pronto!** hello! *(on telephone)*; **pronto intervento** emergency services; **pronto soccorso** first aid

proprietà *f*: **proprietà privata** private property

proprietario(a) *m/f* owner

proprio just; really

proprio(a) own

proroga *f* extension; deferment

prosciutto *m* ham; **prosciutto affumicato** smoked ham; **prosciutto crudo/cotto** raw/cooked ham; **prosciutto di Parma (con melone/fichi)** cured ham from Parma (with melon/figs)

Prosecco *m* dry, sweet white wine with a natural sparkle, from the Trieste area

proseguimento *m*: **volo con proseguimento per ...** flight with onward connection for ...

prossimamente coming soon

prossimo(a) next; **prossima apertura** opening soon

provenienza f origin

provolone m medium-hard white cheese

prugna f plum; **prugne secche** prunes

prurito m itch

PTP abbrev. of **posto telefonico pubblico**

pulitura f: **pulitura a secco** dry cleaning

pulizia f cleaning

pullman m coach

pullmino m minibus

pummarola f: **spaghetti alla pummarola** spaghetti in tomato sauce

punire to punish

punteggio m score

punto m point; spot; stitch; full stop; **punto d'incontro** meeting place; **punto vendita** sales outlet

puntualmente on time

puntura f bite; sting

purè m purée; **purè di patate** mashed potatoes

qua here

quadro m picture; painting

quaglia f quail

qualche some

qualcosa something; anything

qualcuno somebody; anybody

quale what; which; which one

qualsiasi any

qualunque any

quando when

quanto(a) how much; **quanti(e)** how many

quartiere m district; **quartiere popolare** working-class district

quarto m quarter; **un quarto d'ora** quarter of an hour

quarto(a) fourth

quasi nearly; almost

quattro four

quel(la) that

quelli(e) those

quello(a) that

questi(e) these

questo(a) this; this one

questura f police headquarters; police force

qui here

quindi then; therefore

quota f subscription; quota; height; **quota d'iscrizione** enrolment fee; entry fee; membership fee; **quota di partecipazione** cost (of excursion etc)

quotazione f: **quotazione dei cambi** exchange rates

quotidiano m daily (paper)

quotidiano(a) daily

rabarbaro m rhubarb

racchetta f racket; bat; **racchetta da neve** snowshoe; **racchetta da sci** ski stick

raccolta f: **raccolta vetro** bottle bank

raccordo m connection; slip road; **raccordo anulare** ring road

raffreddore *m* cold *(illness)*

ragazza *f* girl; girlfriend

ragazzo *m* boy; boyfriend

ragù *m* : **ragù (di carne)** meat sauce; **ragù vegetale** vegetable sauce

RAI *f* Italian State broadcasting company

rallentare to slow down or up

rame *m* copper

rana *f* frog

rapa *f* turnip

rapido *m* express train

rapido(a) high-speed; quick

rappresentazione *f* performance; production

raso *m* satin

rata *f* instalment

ravanello *m* radish

ravioli *mpl* square cushions of pasta with meat or other filling; **ravioli panna e prosciutto** ravioli with cream and ham

reale royal

recapito *m* address; delivery

recarsi: recarsi alla cassa pay at the cash desk

Recioto *m* sparkling red wine from the Verona area

reclamo *m* complaint

recupero *m* : **recupero monete** returned coins

regalo *m* present; gift

regione *f* region; district; area

Regno Unito *m* United Kingdom

regolamento *m* regulation

regolare regular; steady

remo *m* oar

reparto *m* department *(in store)*; unit

repellente *m* insect repellent

respiratore *m* breathing apparatus

restare to stay; to remain; to be left

restituire to return

restituzione *f* return; repayment; **dietro restituzione dello scontrino** on presentation of the receipt

resto *m* remainder; change

rete *f* net; goal

retro *m* back; **Vedi retro** P.T.O.

ribes *m* blackcurrant

ricambio *m* : **ricambi auto** car spares; **ricambi originali** car manufacturers' spare parts

ricetta *f* prescription; recipe

ricevere to receive; to welcome; **si riceve solo per appuntamento** visits by appointment only

ricevimento *m* reception; reception desk

ricevitore *m* receiver *(phone)*

ricevuta *f* receipt; **ricevuta di ritorno** acknowledgement of receipt; **ricevuta fiscale** receipt *(for tax purposes)*

riconoscimento *m* : **documento di riconoscimento** means of identification

ricordo *m* souvenir; memory

ricorrere a to resort to

ricotta *f* soft white unsalted cheese

riduzione *f* reduction

rientro *m* return; return home

rifare to do again; to repair

rifiutare to refuse; to reject

rifiuti *mpl* rubbish; waste

rifornimento *m* : **posto di rifornimento** filling station

rifugio *m* refuge; shelter

riguardo *m* care; respect; **riguardo a ...** as regards ...

rilascio *m* : **data di rilascio** date of issue

rimanere to stay; to remain; to be left

rimborso *m* refund; **rimborso spese mediche a seguito infortunio** refund of medical expenses following an accident

rimessa *f* remittance; garage

rimorchio *m* trailer; **a rimorchio** on tow

rimozione *f* : **divieto di parcheggio con zona rimozione** no parking: offenders' cars will be towed away; **rimozione forzata** illegally parked cars will be towed away

rincrescere: **mi rincresce che ...** I regret that ...

rinfreschi *mpl* refreshments

ringraziare to thank

rinnovare to renew

rinunce *fpl* cancellations

rinunciare to give up

riparazione *f* repair

ripido(a) abrupt; steep

ripieno *m* stuffing

ripieno(a) stuffed; filled

risalita *f* : **impianto di risalita** ski lift(s)

risarcimento *m* compensation

riscaldamento *m* heating

rischio *m* risk; **il bagaglio viaggia a rischio e pericolo del partecipante** luggage is carried at owner's risk

risciacquare ro rinse

riscuotere to collect; to cash

riserva *f* reserve; reservation; **riserva di caccia** game reserve; **riserva naturale** nature reserve

riservare to reserve

riservato(a) reserved

risi e bisi *mpl* rice and peas cooked in chicken stock

riso *m* laugh; rice; **riso in bianco** boiled rice with butter; **riso alla greca** rice salad with olives

risotto *m* dish of rice cooked in stock with various ingredients; **risotto ai funghi/alla marinara** risotto with mushrooms/fish; **risotto alla milanese** risotto with saffron and Parmesan cheese; **risotto nero alla fiorentina** risotto with cuttlefish, garlic, white wine

rispondere to answer; to reply; to respond

ristorante *m* restaurant

ristorazione *f* : **servizi di ristorazione** refreshments

ristoro *m* : **servizio ristoro** refreshments

ritardo *m* delay; **essere in ritardo** to be late

ritirare to withdraw

ritirata *f* WC

ritiro *m* retirement; withdrawal; **ritiro bagagli** baggage claim

ritorno *m* return

riva *f* bank

rivedere to see again; to revise

rivendita *f* resale; retailer's shop

riviera *f* : **la Riviera ligure** the Italian Riviera

rivista f magazine; revue
roba f stuff; belongings
roccia f rock
rognone m kidney
rompere to break
rosso(a) red
rosticceria f shop selling roast meat and other prepared food
rotonda f roundabout
rotondo(a) round
roulotte f caravan
rovina f ruin
ruota f wheel; **ruota di scorta** spare wheel
ruscello m stream

sabato m Saturday
sabbioso(a) sandy
sacchetto m (small) bag
sacco m bag; sack; **sacco a pelo** sleeping bag
sala f hall; auditorium; **sala d'aspetto/d'attesa** waiting room; airport lounge; **sala da gioco** gaming room; **sala giochi** games room; **sala di lettura** reading room; **sala TV** TV lounge
salato(a) salted; salty; savoury
saldare to settle (bill); to weld
saldi mpl sales (cheap prices)
saldo m payment; balance
sale m salt; **sale fino** table salt; **sale grosso** cooking salt; **sali e tabacchi** tobacconist's shop
salire to rise; to go up
salita f climb; slope; **in salita** uphill
salmì m game stewed in a rich brown sauce

salmone m salmon; **salmone affumicato** smoked salmon
salone m lounge; salon; **salone di bellezza** beauty salon; **salone di ritrovo** lounge
salotto m living room; sitting room
salsa f gravy; sauce; **salsa di pomodoro** tomato sauce; **salsa rubra** ketchup; **salsa tartara** tartare sauce; **salsa verde** sauce made with parsley, anchovy fillets, gherkins, potato, garlic and onion
salsiccia f sausage
saltato(a) sautéed
saltimbocca m : **saltimbocca (alla romana)** veal escalopes with ham, sage and white wine
salumeria f delicatessen
salumi mpl cured pork meats
salute f health
saluto m greeting
salvagente pedonale m traffic island
salvia f sage
salvo except; unless; **salvo imprevisti** barring accidents
sangue m blood; **al sangue** rare (steak)
sanguinaccio m black pudding
Sangiovese m dry red table wine from Emilia-Romagna
sanzioni fpl sanctions
sapone m soap; **sapone da barba** shaving soap
sapore m flavour; taste
saporito(a) tasty
sarago m bream
sarde fpl sardines (usually cooked

in olive oil and oregano)

Sardegna f Sardinia

sardella f pilchard

sartoria f tailor's; dressmaker's

sasso m stone

sbaglio m mistake

sbarco m : **al momento dello sbarco**
on landing

sbrigare: sbrigare le formalità to
deal with the formalities

scadenza f expiry

scadere to expire

scaduto(a) out-of-date

scala f scale; ladder; staircase; **scala
mobile** escalator

scaldabagno m water heater

scaldare to warm

scale fpl stairs

scalinata f flight of steps

scalino m step

scalo m stopover

scaloppa f: **scaloppa milanese** veal
escalope fried in egg and
breadcrumbs

scaloppina f veal escalope;
scaloppine al limone/al Marsala veal
escalopes in a lemon/Marsala
sauce

scampi mpl : **scampi ai ferri** grilled
scampi; **code di scampi dorati e
fritti** scampi tails, breaded and
fried

scampoli mpl remnants

scapolo m bachelor

scarico(a) flat (battery)

scarpa f shoe

scarpone da sci m ski boot

scatolame m tinned food; tins

scatto m (telephone) unit

scelta f range; selection; choice

scendere to go down

scheda f slip (of paper); **vendita
schede telefoniche** phonecards sold
here

schermo m screen

schiacciare to mash

schiena f back

schienale m back (of chair);
**mantenere lo schienale in posizione
eretta** ensure your seat back is in
the upright position

schiuma f foam

sci m ski; skiing; **sci accompagnato**
skiing with instructors; **sci di fondo**
cross-country skiing; **sci nautico or
d'acqua** water-skiing

scialuppa di salvataggio f lifeboat

sciare to ski

sciatore(trice) m/f skier

sciopero m strike

sciovia f ski lift

**sciroppato(a): prugne/ciliegie
sciroppate** plums/cherries in syrup

sciroppo m syrup; **sciroppo per la
tosse** cough mixture

scogliera f cliff

scolapiatti m draining-board

scompartimento m compartment

scongelare to defrost

scontabile: tariffa non scontabile no
discount on this rate

sconto m discount; **non si fanno
sconti** no discounts given

scontrino m ticket; receipt; **esigete
lo scontrino** ask for a receipt;
scontrino alla cassa pay at the cash

desk first and bring your receipt to the bar; **scontrino fiscale** receipt for tax purposes

scorciatoia f short cut

scorcio m glimpse; **scorcio panoramico** vista

scottatura f burn; sunburn

Scozia f Scotland

scozzese Scottish

scrivere to write

scuola f school

scusarsi to apologise

sdrucciolevole slippery

se if; whether

sé oneself

secco(a) dried; dry

secolo m century

secondo(a) second; according to; **di seconda mano** secondhand

sedano m celery

sede f seat; head office

sedersi to sit down

sedia f chair; **sedia a sdraio** deckchair

seggiolone m highchair

seggiovia f chair-lift

segnalazione f: **segnalazioni guasti** reporting of faults

segnale m signal; road sign; **segnale di linea libera** dial(ling) tone

segnaletica f road signs; **segnaletica orizzontale in rifacimento** road markings being renewed

segreteria f secretary's office; **segreteria telefonica** answering service

seguente following

seguire to follow; to continue

sei six

selvaggina f game (hunting)

selz m soda water

semaforo m traffic lights

semifreddo m chilled dessert made with ice cream

semola f: **semola di grano duro** durum wheat

semolino m: **semolino al latte** semolina pudding

semplice plain; simple

sempre always; ever

senape f mustard

senso m sense; **strada a senso unico** one-way street

sentiero m path; footpath

senza without

seppia f cuttlefish; **seppie in umido** stewed cuttlefish

seppioline fpl baby cuttlefish

sera f evening

serata f: **serata di gala** gala evening

serra f greenhouse

servizio m service; service charge; report (in press); **servizi** facilities; bathroom; **in servizio** in use; on duty; **fuori servizio** out of order; off duty; **servizio interurbano/ internazionale con prenotazione** booking service for long-distance/international calls; **servizio al tavolo** waiter/waitress service; **servizi igienici** bathroom fittings; **camera con servizi privati** room with private bathroom

seta f silk

sette seven

settembre m September

settentrionale northern

settimana f week; **settimana bianca** week's skiing holiday

sfogliatelle fpl flaky pastry filled with cream cheese and fruit

sfuso(a) loose; on tap (wine)

sganciarsi: sganciarsi adesso let go of the bar now

sgombro m mackerel

sì yes

Sicilia f Sicily

sicurezza f safety; security

sidro m cider

sigaretta f cigarette

sigaro m cigar

Signor ® m Mr

signora f lady; madam; **Signora** Mrs

signore m gentleman; sir

signorina f young woman; miss

silenzio m silence

simpatico(a) pleasant; nice

singola f single room

singolo(a) single

sinistra f left

SIP f Italian telephone company

sistemazione f: **sistemazione alberghiera** hotel accommodation

sito m site

skai ® m Leatherette ®

slacciare to unfasten; to undo

slavina f snowslide

slitta f sledge; sleigh

smoking m dinner jacket

Soave m dry white wine from the Verona area

sobborgo m suburb

soccorso m assistance; **soccorso pubblico di emergenza** emergency police service

socio m associate; member

sodo hard; hard-boiled

soffice soft

sofficini mpl small savoury fritters

soffitto m ceiling

soggiorno m visit; stay; sitting room; **soggiorno balneare** stay at the seaside

sogliola f sole; **sogliola ai ferri** grilled sole; **sogliola alla mugnaia** sole lightly fried in butter with lemon juice and parsley

solamente only

solare solar; **crema/olio solare** suntan cream/oil

sole m sun; sunshine

sollevare to raise; to relieve

sollievo m relief

solo only

solubile soluble; **caffè solubile** instant coffee

sonnifero m sleeping pill

soppressata f type of sausage

soppresso(a): corsa soppressa nei giorni festivi no service on holidays

sopra on; above; over; on top

soprattassa f surcharge

sorella f sister

sorgente f spring

sorvegliante m/f supervisor

sospensione f: **sospensione voli** flights postponed

sospeso(a): corsa sospesa service cancelled

sosta f stop; **divieto di sosta/sosta**

vietata no waiting

sostanzioso(a) filling; nourishing

sostare: vietato sostare nei passaggi di intercomunicazione do not stand in the passageway

sostitutivo(a): servizio sostitutivo con autocorsa back-up coach service

sottaceti *mpl* pickles

sotterraneo(a) underground

sottile thin; fine; subtle

sotto underneath; under; below

sottopassaggio *m* underpass

sottotitolo *m* subtitle

spaccio *m* shop

spaghetti *mpl* : **spaghetti all' amatriciana** spaghetti in tomato sauce with garlic and Parmesan cheese; **spaghetti alla bolognese** spaghetti in a meat and tomato sauce; **spaghetti alla carbonara** spaghetti with bacon, eggs and Parmesan cheese; **spaghetti alla ciociara** spaghetti with black olives, tomatoes, peppers and cheese; **spaghetti al pomodoro** spaghetti in tomato sauce; **spaghetti alle vongole** spaghetti with clams

spalmare to spread

spartitraffico *m* central reservation

spazzaneve *m* snowplough

specificare to specify

spedalità *f* hospital admissions office; hospital expenses

spedire to send; to dispatch; to ship

spegnere to turn off; to put out

spesa *f* expense

spese *fpl* expenditure; expenses; costs

spesso often

spettacolo *m* show; performance

spezie *fpl* spices

spezzatino *m* stew; **carni bianche in spezzatino** poultry stew

spia *f* spy; warning light; **con la spia spenta non selezionate** do not use when light is out

spiacente sorry

spiacere = dispiacere

spiaggia *f* beach; shore; **spiaggia libera** public beach

spiccioli *mpl* (small) change

spiedino *m* skewer; **spiedini di calamari** squid kebabs

spiedo *m* spit

spiegazione *f* explanation

spina *f* bone *(of fish)*; plug *(electric)*; **togliere la spina** remove the plug

spinaci *mpl* spinach

spingere to push; **spingere i carrelli all'uscita** please leave trolleys at the exit

spogliarello *m* striptease

spogliatoio *m* dressing room

sporgersi: è pericoloso sporgersi it is dangerous to lean out

sportello *m* counter; window; door *(of car)*; **servizio sportelli automatici** automatic banking service

sposato(a) married

spremuta *f* : **spremuta d'arancia/di limone/di pompelmo** fresh orange/lemon/grapefruit juice

spuma *f* foam; fizzy drink; **spuma di tonno** tuna mousse

spumante sparkling

spuntino m snack

sputare to spit

S.r.l. Ltd

stabilimento m factory;
stabilimento balneare bathing
establishment

stadio m stadium

stagionato(a) ripe; mature

stagione f season

stagno m pond

stagnola f tin foil

stalla f stable

stampatello m block letters

stampigliatura f : **non è valido senza
la stampigliatura** not valid unless
stamped

stanza f room; **stanza da bagno**
bathroom; **stanza doppia/a due letti**
doubled/twin-bedded room; **stanza
da letto** bedroom; **stanza
matrimoniale** double room; **stanza
degli ospiti** guest room; **stanza
singola** single room

stasera tonight

Stati Uniti (d'America) mpl
United States (of America)

stazione f station; resort; **stazione
autocorriere** coach station; **stazione
balneare** seaside resort; **stazione
marittima** seaside town; **stazione di
servizio** petrol station; **stazione
termale** spa

stecchino m toothpick; wooden
skewer; **stecchini alla bolognese**
chicken livers, sweetbreads etc,
skewered with bread and cheese
and cooked in a white sauce

sterlina f sterling; pound

stesso(a) same

stinco m shin

stitichezza f constipation

stoccafisso m stockfish

storico(a) historic(al)

storione m sturgeon

stoviglie fpl crockery

stracchino m soft, creamy cheese

stracciatella f clear soup with eggs
and cheese stirred in; chocolate-
chip ice-cream

stracotto m beef stew

strada f road; street; **strada
panoramica** scenic route; **strada
principale** main road; **strada
sbarrata** road closed; **strada
secondaria** side road, side street;
strada statale main road, **strada a
doppia carreggiata** dual
carriageway; **strada con diritto di
precedenza** on this road you have
right of way; **strada senza uscita**
dead end

straniero(a) foreign; overseas;
foreigner

strappare to tear; to rip; to pull off

stretto(a) narrow; tight

stretto m strait (sea)

stufato m stew

stufato(a) braised

stuoia f mat

stuzzichino m appetizer

su on; onto; over; about; up

sua his; her(s); its; your(s)

subacqueo(a) underwater

subito at once

succo m juice; **succo di frutta** fruit
juice

succursale f branch

sud *m* south

sue his; her(s); its; your(s)

sugo *m* sauce; gravy; juice

suino(a): carni suine *fpl* pork meats

suo(i) his; her(s); its; your(s)

suonare to ring; to play; to sound

superare to exceed; to pass; to overtake

supermercato *m* supermarket

supplemento *m* : **supplemento singola** supplement for single room

supposta *f* suppository

surgelato(a): prodotti surgelati frozen foods

susina *f* plum

sveglia *f* alarm (clock)

sviluppo *m* : **sviluppo rapido** fast developing service *(photos)*; **sviluppo e stampa** developing and printing

svincolo *m* slip road

Svizzera *f* Switzerland

svizzero(a): (bistecca alla) svizzera *f* ≈ beefburger

svolta *f* turn

T ground floor; **T sali e tabacchi** tobacconist's (shop)

tabaccaio(a) *m/f* tobacconist's

tabaccheria *f* tobacconist's (shop)

tabacco *m* tobacco; **tabacchi** tobacconist's (shop)

tacchino *m* turkey

tacco *m* heel

taccole *fpl* mange-tout peas

taglia *f* size *(of clothes)*; **taglie forti** larger sizes

tagliatelle *fpl* flat strips of pasta

taglierini *mpl* thin soup noodles

taglio *m* cut

tale such

taleggio *m* mild, medium-hard cheese

tanti(e) so many

tanto(a) so much; so

tappa *f* stop; stage

tardi late

tariffa *f* tariff; rate; **tariffa doganale** customs tariff; **tariffa festiva** rate on holidays; **tariffa normale/ridotta** standard/reduced rate; **tariffa notturna** night rate; **tariffa ordinaria/a ore di punta** ordinary/peak rate

tartufo *m* truffle; chocolate truffle

tassa *f* tax; **tassa d'ingresso** admission charge; **tassa di soggiorno** tourist tax; **tasse e percentuali di servizio** taxes and service charge

tassì *m* taxi

tasso *m* rate; **tasso di cambio** exchange rate

tavola *f* table; plank; board; painting; **tavola calda** snack bar; **tavola a vela** windsurfing board

tè *m* tea; **tè al limone/al latte** tea with lemon/milk; **tè freddo** iced tea

teatro *m* theatre; drama

tedesco(a) German

tegame *m* (frying) pan; **patate in tegame** potatoes with peppers, onion, tomato and oregano

telefonata *f* phone-call

telefono *m* telephone

teleselezione *f* S.T.D.

televisore *m* television *(set)*

temperatura *f* : **temperatura ambiente** room temperature

tempio *m* temple

tempo *m* weather; time

temporale *m* thunderstorm

tenda *f* curtain; tent; **tenda canadese** ridge tent

tenere to keep; to hold; **tenere rigorosamente la destra** keep to the right

tenero(a) tender

tenore *m* : **tenore alcolico** alcohol content

tensione *f* voltage; tension

tenuta *f* estate *(property)*

terme *fpl* thermal baths

terrazza *f* terrace

terzi *mpl* third party

terzo(a) third

tesoro *m* treasure

tessera *f* (membership) card; pass; season ticket

testa *f* head

testina *f* : **testina di abbacchio/vitello** lamb's/calf's head

tettoia *f* shelter

Tevere *m* Tiber

ticket *m* prescription charge

timballo *m* mixture of meat, fish etc cooked in a mould lined with pastry or potato

timbro *m* (rubber) stamp

timo *m* thyme

tinca *f* tench

tintoria *f* dry-cleaner's

tintura *f* dye; rinse *(for hair)*; **tintura**

di iodio tincture of iodine

tiramisù *m* coffee-flavoured sponge cake filled with cream cheese, eggs, sugar, cream, and covered with chocolate

tirare to pull

tiro *m* : **tiro con l'arco** archery

Tocai *m* dry white wine from Friuli

toccare to touch; to feel

togliere to remove; to take away

tomba *f* grave; tomb

tonno *m* tuna

torcicollo *m* stiff neck

Torino *f* Turin

tornare to return; to come/go back

torre *f* tower

torrefazione *f* coffee shop

torrone *m* nougat

torta *f* cake; tart; pie; **torta di gelato** ice-cream cake; **torta di riso** rice mould; **torta salata** savoury tart

tortellini *mpl* pasta rings filled with seasoned meat; **tortellini in brodo** tortellini in broth

tortello *m* pasta ring filled with spinach and cream cheese

tortellone *m* pasta ring filled with cheese, egg, parsley and cream cheese

Toscana *f* Tuscany

tosse *f* cough

tosti *mpl* toasted sandwiches

Totip *m* similar to football pools, but for horse-racing

Totocalcio *m* football pools

tra between; among(st); in

tracciato *m* : **posteggio limitatamente entro i tracciati**

parking only within area indicated

traduzione *f* translation

traghetto *m* ferry

traguardo *m* finishing line

tramezzino *m* sandwich

tramonto *m* sunset

trampolino *m* diving-board

tranne except (for)

tranquillante *m* tranquillizer

transito *m* : **transito voli nazionali/internazionali** domestic/international transit passengers

trascorrere to pass; to spend

trasferibile transferable

trasgressore *m* : **i trasgressori saranno assoggettati alla penalità di ...** offenders will be subject to a fine of ...

trasporto *m* transport; **trasporto consentito con biglietto preacquistato** bus tickets must be purchased before boarding

trasversale *f* : **(strada) trasversale** side street

tratto *m* : **tratto di linea interrotto per lavori** section of the line closed due to maintenance work

traversata *f* crossing; flight

tre three

trenette *fpl* strips of pasta, similar to **tagliatelle**

treno *m* train; **treno merci** goods train; **treno navetta** alpine train for the transport of cars and their passengers; **treno periodico** train which operates only during certain periods; **treni in partenza** train departures

tribunale *m* law court

triglia *f* mullet

trippa *f* tripe

tritare to mince; to chop

troppi(e) too many

troppo too much; too

troppo(a) too much

trota *f* trout; **trota ai ferri** grilled trout; **trota alla valdostana** poached trout in a butter sauce

trovare to find

tu you

tubo *m* pipe; tube

tuffo *m* dive

turno *m* turn; shift; **di turno** on duty; **chiuso per turno (di riposo) il lunedì** closed on Mondays

tutti(e) all; everybody; **tutte le direzioni** through traffic

tutto everything

tutto(a) all

ubicazione *f* location

ufficio *m* bureau; office; church service; **ufficio informazioni** information office; **ufficio oggetti smarriti** lost property office; **ufficio postale** post office; **ufficio turistico** tourist office

uguale equal; even

ultimo(a) last

umidi *mpl* stews

umido(a) wet; damp; **carne/pesce in umido** meat/fish stew

un a; an; one

unguento *m* ointment

unità sanitaria locale *f* local health centre

uno(a) a; an; one; **l'un l'altro** one another

uomo (*pl* **uomini**) *m* man

uovo *m* egg; **uovo al burro** egg fried in butter; **uovo in camicia/alla coque** poached/boiled egg; **uovo fritto/ripieno/sodo** fried/stuffed/hard-boiled egg; **uova in frittata** omelette; **uova in strapazzata** scrambled eggs

uragano *m* hurricane

uscire to come out; to go out; **vietato uscire dalla pista** follow the piste *(skiing)*

uscita *f* exit; **uscita operai** factory exit; **uscita di sicurezza** emergency exit; **uscita a vela** sailing trip

USL *abbrev. of* **unità sanitaria locale**

uso *m* use

utile useful

uva *f* grapes; **uva passa** currants; raisins; **uva spina** gooseberry

va: Lei va you go; **lui va** he goes

vacanza *f* holiday(s)

vaglia *m* postal order; money order

vagone *m* carriage; wagon; **vagone letto** sleeping car; **vagone ristorante** restaurant car

valanga *f* avalanche

valico *m* pass; **valico di confine** border crossing

validare to make valid

valido: valido fino a ... valid until ...

valigia *f* suitcase

valle *f* valley

Valpolicella *m* light, dry red wine with a trace of bitterness

valuta *f* currency

valvola *f* valve

vaniglia *f* vanilla

vano *m* room

vantaggioso(a): a condizioni vantaggiose on favourable terms

vasca da bagno *f* bath

vassoio *m* tray

vecchio(a) old

vedere to see

veduta *f* view

veicolo *m* vehicle

vela *f* sail; sailing

veleno *m* poison

velluto *m* velvet

veloce fast

velocità *f* speed

vendere to sell; **vendesi** for sale; **qui si vende ...** ... sold here

vendita *f* sale; **vendita al minuto** retail; **vendita promozionale** special offer; **vendita a rate** hire purchase

venerdì *m* Friday; **venerdì santo** Good Friday

Venezia *f* Venice

venire to come

vento *m* wind

ventola *f* fan

verde green

Verdicchio *m* dry white wine from the Marche

verdura *f* vegetables

Verduzzo *m* dry white wine

vermicelli *mpl* : **vermicelli alle vongole veraci** thin noodles with real clams

vermut *m* vermouth

Vernaccia *m* dry or sweet white wine

vernice *f* paint; **vernice fresca** wet paint

vero(a) true; real

versamento *m* payment; deposit

verso toward(s)

vestibolo *m* hall

vettura *f* coach *(of train)*

vi you; yourselves; each other; there

via¹ *f* street

via² by way of

viaggiare to travel

viaggiatore *m* traveller

viaggio *m* journey; trip; drive; **viaggi** travel; **viaggio organizzato** package holiday

viale *m* avenue

vicino near; close by

vicolo *m* alley; lane; **vicolo cieco** dead end

vietato(a) forbidden; **vietato calpestare l'erba** do not walk on the grass; **vietato fumare** no smoking; **vietato scendere** no exit; **vietato sputare** no spitting; **vietato l'ingresso** no entry; **vietato l'ingresso alle persone sprovviste di biglietto di viaggio** ticket-holders only beyond this point

vigile *m* policeman; **vigili del fuoco** fire brigade; **vigile urbano** traffic warden

vigilia *f* eve

vigna *f* vineyard

villaggio *m*: **villaggio vacanze** holiday village

villeggiante *m/f* holidaymaker

villeggiatura *f*: **in villeggiatura** on holiday

vincolo *m*: **senza alcun vincolo** without obligation

vino *m* wine; **vino bianco/rosso/rosato or rosé** white/red/rosé wine; **vini da pasto** table wines; **vini pregiati** quality wines; **vini da taglio** blending wines

Vin Santo *m* golden-coloured dessert wine from Tuscany

vipera *f* adder

visione *f* vision; **cinema di prima visione** cinema where new-release films are shown

visita *f* visit; **visita guidata** guided tour

viso *m* face

vista *f* eyesight; view; **camera con vista mare** room with sea view

visto *m* visa; **visto di ingresso/di transito** entry/transit visa

visualizzatore *m*: **nel visualizzatore si accenderà la lampadina rossa** the red light will show on the display

vita *f* life; waist; **vita notturna** night life

vite *f* vine; screw

vitello *m* veal; calf; **vitello tonnato** veal in tuna fish sauce, served cold

vivande *fpl* food

vivere to live

vivo(a) live; alive

volano *m* badminton

volo *m* flight; **volo di linea** scheduled flight; **volo provenienza...** flight from...

volta *f* time; **una volta** once

voltare to turn
vongola *f* clam
vostro(a) your; yours
Vostri(e) your; yours
vuoto(a) empty

zabaglione/zabaione *m* whipped egg yolks and sugar with Marsala wine
zafferano *m* saffron
zampone *m* pig's trotter stuffed with minced pork and spices
zanzara *f* mosquito
zenzero *m* ginger
zia *f* aunt(ie)
zio *m* uncle
zona *f* zone; **zona pedonale** pedestrian precinct; **zona residenziale** housing estate
zucca *f* pumpkin; marrow
zucchero *m* sugar
zucchini *mpl* courgettes; **zucchini in agrodolce** courgettes in a sweet and sour sauce; **zucchini in teglia** baked courgettes with onions and Parmesan cheese
zuccotto *m* ice-cream sponge
zuppa *f* soup; **zuppa di cipolle** onion soup; **zuppa di pesce** fish soup; **zuppa inglese** a sort of trifle

NOTES